Great Patchwork: Working with Triangles

BETTER HOMES AND GARDENS®

Great Patchwork:
Working with Triangles

BETTER HOMES AND GARDENS® BOOKS

DES MOINES, IOWA

Better Homes and Gardens® Books, an imprint of Meredith® Books:
President, Book Group: Joseph J. Ward
Vice President, Editorial Director: Elizabeth P. Rice

Executive Editor: Maryanne Bannon
Senior Editor: Carol Spier
Associate Editor: Carolyn Mitchell
Selections Editor: Eleanor Levie
Editorial Coordinator: Sandra Choron, March Tenth, Inc.
Technical Director: Cyndi Marsico
Book Design: Beth Tondreau Design
Technical Artist: Phoebe Gaughan
Photographer: Steven Mays
Photo Stylist: Susan Piatt
Production Manager: Bill Rose

Cover photographed in: The Darien Historical Society

The editors would like to thank James and Judith Milne Antiques, and
Laura Fisher Antiques, both in New York City, for their kind assistance
in the search for quilts to include in this volume.

ISBN: 0-696-00087-3
Library of Congress Catalog Card Number: 93-080853

Printed in the United States of America
10 9 8 7 6 5 4 3 2 1

All of us at Better Homes and Gardens® Books are dedicated to offering you,
our customer, the best books we can create. We are particularly concerned that all
of our instructions for making projects are clear and accurate.
Please address your correspondence to Customer Service, Meredith® Press,
150 East 52nd Street, New York, NY 10022.

If you would like to order additional copies of any of our books,
call 1-800-678-2803 or check with your local bookstore.

Contents

The quilt designs in this book all use triangles as their primary geometric unit. As the points of the triangles turn and intersect, all sorts of beautiful—and sometimes lively—patterns emerge. Re-create the patterns as shown, or work out a personal version by using the **CHANGING COLORS** and **CHANGING SETS** directions that accompany each project. If you are new to making patchwork with triangles, begin with the Triangles-in-Triangles Runner or the Starry Path Pillow. If you are shy about experimenting with color, begin with the small Winter Storm Warning Wallhanging, which invites your own interpretation of the sky. And if you are very sure of your quilting skills, accept our **EXPERT'S CHALLENGE**— or if you are not yet an expert, just enjoy and marvel over this quilt's brilliance.

These symbols, found on the opening page of each project, identify suggested levels of experience needed to make the projects in this book. However, you will see within these pages many interpretations of each project, and the editors hope you will find in each chapter something easily achievable or challenging, as you wish.

 New Quilter   Confident Quilter    Expert Quilter

Dutchman's Puzzle/ Yankee Puzzle Quilt

BY MARGARET B. BREHMER

This quilt was made to celebrate the marriage and move to the Netherlands of a young American friend of the quilter's. Both the blocks have pinwheel centers; the Dutchman's Puzzle, made with large and small triangles, seems to have windmill blades, while the color arrangement of the Yankee Puzzle gives the appearance of a sawtooth border.

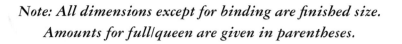

Note: All dimensions except for binding are finished size.
Amounts for full/queen are given in parentheses.

DUTCHMAN'S PUZZLE BLOCK
21 (45) blocks, 7″ square

PLAIN BLOCK
40 (84) blocks, 7″ square

YANKEE PUZZLE BLOCK
20 (40) blocks, 7″ square

FIRST BORDER
4 strips, 1¾″ wide, cut to size

SECOND BORDER
4 strips, ½″ wide, cut to size

THIRD BORDER
4 strips, 3½″ wide, cut to size

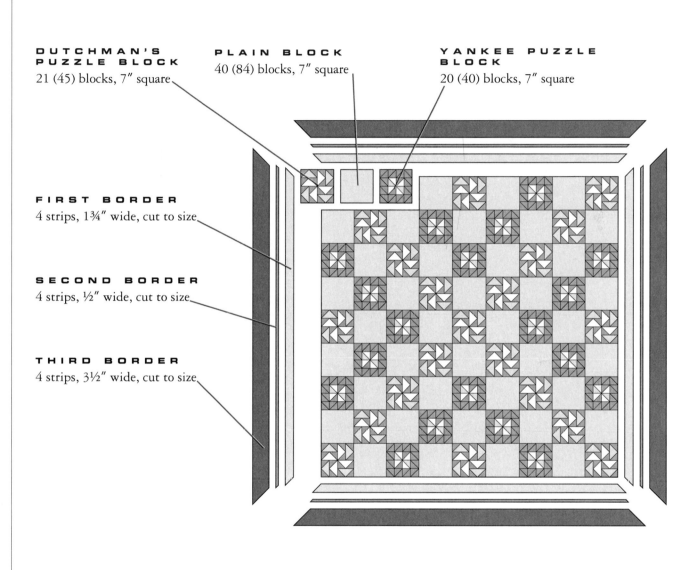

BINDING
1½″-wide strip, pieced as necessary and cut to size

Note: Sizes and amounts for full/queen are given in parentheses.

Yardages are based on 44" fabric. Prepare templates, if desired, referring to drafting schematics. Cut strips and patches following schematics and chart (see "Using the Cutting Charts," page 91). Cut binding as directed below. Except for drafting schematics, which give finished sizes, all dimensions include ¼" seam allowance and strips include extra length, unless otherwise stated. (NOTE: Angles on all patches are either 45° or 90°.)

DIMENSIONS

FINISHED BLOCK
7" square, about 9⅞" diagonal

FINISHED QUILT
73½" (101") square

MATERIALS

- **ANTIQUE WHITE PRINT**
  2½ (3¾) yds.

- **LT. GRAPE PRINT**
  5¾ (8¾) yds.

- **MED. GREEN PRINT**
  ¾ (1½) yds.

- **DK. GREEN PRINT**
  ¾ (1½) yds.

- **ROYAL BLUE PRINT**
  ¾ (1½) yds.

- **MED. GRAPE PRINT**
  1¼ (2¼) yds.

- **DK. GRAPE PRINT**
  ¾ (1½) yds.

- **DK. RED-PURPLE PRINT**
  3 (4) yds.

- **PURPLE FLORAL**
  2½ (3) yds.

- **BACKING ***
  5½ (9½) yds.

- **BATTING ***

- **THREAD**

- **BINDING**
  Use ½ yd. lt. grape print to make a 1½" × 320" (1½" × 430") strip.

*Backing and batting should be cut and pieced as necessary so they are at least 4" larger than quilt top on all sides, then trimmed to size after quilting.

DRAFTING SCHEMATICS

(No seam allowance added)

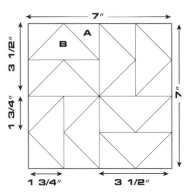

DUTCHMAN'S PUZZLE BLOCK

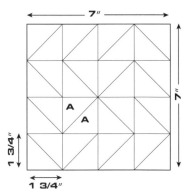

YANKEE PUZZLE BLOCK

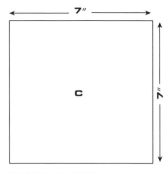

PLAIN BLOCK

CUTTING SCHEMATICS

(Seam allowance included)

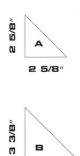

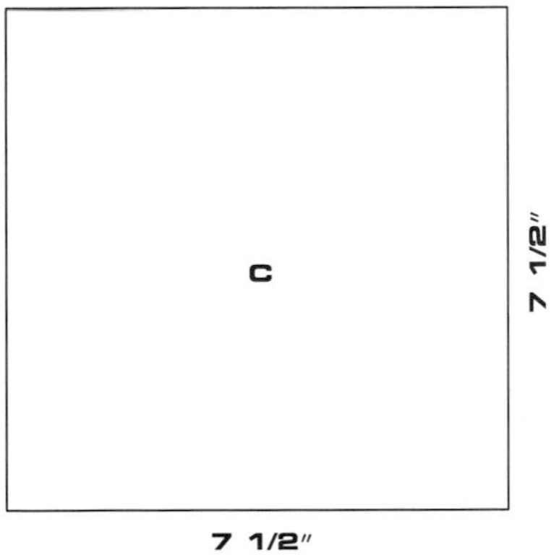

2 5/8" A 2 5/8"

3 3/8" B 3 3/8"

C

7 1/2" 7 1/2"

Fabric and Yardage	FIRST CUT		SECOND CUT		Shape
	Number of Pieces	Size	Number of Pieces		
			For 40 (84) Plain Blocks	For 21 (45) Dutchman's Puzzle Blocks	
PLAIN PATCHES					
Med. Green ¼ (½) yd.	2 (3)	2⅝" × 40"	–	42 (90)	A
Dk. Green ¼ (½) yd.	2 (3)	2⅝" × 40"	–	42 (90)	A
Royal Blue ¼ (½) yd.	2 (3)	2⅝" × 40"	–	42 (90)	A
Med. Grape ¼ (½) yd.	2 (3)	2⅝" × 40"	–	42 (90)	A
Dk. Grape ¼ (½) yd.	2 (3)	2⅝" × 40"	–	42 (90)	A
Red-Purple[1] 2¼ (3) yds.	1 (2)	2⅝" × 80"	–	42 (90)	A
SECOND BORDER					
	4	1⅞" × 78" (1⅞" × 106")			
Antique White ½ (1) yd.	4 (9)	3⅜" × 40"	–	84 (180)	B
Lt. Grape 4½ (7) yds.	2 (5)	3⅜" × 80"	–	84 (180)	B
	8 (17)	7½" × 40"	40 (84)	–	C
FIRST BORDER					
	4	2¼" × 77" (2¼" × 105")			
Purple Floral 2½ (3) yds. **THIRD BORDER**					
	4	4" × 84" (4" × 106")			

[1] Reserve remainder of fabric for cutting triangle squares.

| | FIRST CUT | | SECOND CUT | |
Fabric and Yardage	Number of Pieces	Size	Number of Pieces For 20 (40) Yankee Puzzle Blocks	Shape
SPEEDY TRIANGLE SQUARES[1]				
Antique White and Lt. Grape ¾ (1¼) yd. each	2 (4)	8⅞" × 19⅜"	40 (80)	A/A[2] ◨
Antique White and Med. Grape ½ (¾) yd. each	1 (2)	8⅞" × 19⅜"	20 (40)	A/A[3] ◨
Antique White and Red-Purple ½ (¾) yd. each	1 (2)	8⅞" × 19⅜"	20 (40)	A/A[4] ◨
Assorted Green/ Blue/Grape Prints ½ (1) yd. each	6 (12)	14¾" × 19⅜"	480 (960)	A/A[5] ◨

[1] See Speedy Triangle Squares (page 93).
[2] Mark 3 × 7 grids with 2⅝" squares.
[3] Mark 3 × 7 grids with 2⅝" squares.
[4] Mark 3 × 7 grids with 2⅝" squares. Use remainder of red-purple from border strips and plain patches.
[5] Mark 6 × 7 grids with 2⅝" squares. Use 6 (12) different medium/dark combinations.

ADJUSTING THE SIZE

This quilt can be enlarged from twin to full/queen by increasing the number of blocks to make two additional rows on each side, continuing the overall pattern formed by the blocks, and increasing the length of the border strips to fit. Refer to the cutting charts, *preceding page and above*, for the number of pieces to cut for the different sizes.

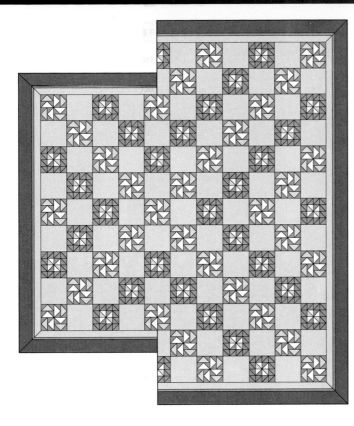

TWIN
40 plain blocks, 21 Dutchman's Puzzle blocks, 20 Yankee Puzzle blocks, quilt center 63″ square

FULL/QUEEN
84 plain blocks, 45 Dutchman's Puzzle blocks, 40 Yankee Puzzle blocks, quilt center 91″ square

BLOCK ASSEMBLY

Dutchman's Puzzle Block

Directions are given below for making one whole block. Amounts for making all 21 (twin) or 45 (full/queen) whole blocks at the same time are given in parentheses.

COLOR KEY
☐ Antique white print
☐ Lt. grape print
▨ Assorted green/blue/grape prints
■ Purple floral

1. Sew 2 different assorted A's to each B to make 4 (84) (180) white/assorted and 4 (84) (180) lt. grape/assorted rectangles.

2. Join rectangles in pairs to make 4 (84) (180) quarter-blocks.

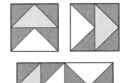

3. Arrange quarter-blocks as shown. Join quarter-blocks.

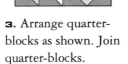

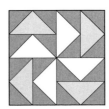

FINISHED DUTCHMAN'S PUZZLE BLOCK

Yankee Puzzle Block

Arrange A/A squares as shown to make 4 rows. Join rows.

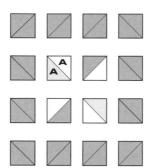

FINISHED YANKEE PUZZLE BLOCK

Quilt Center

Arrange units as shown. Join units to make rows. Join rows.

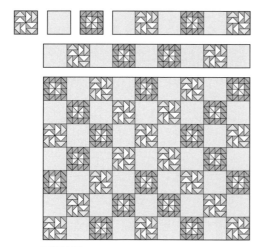

TWIN

FULL/QUEEN

Borders

Join borders to quilt center, mitering corners.

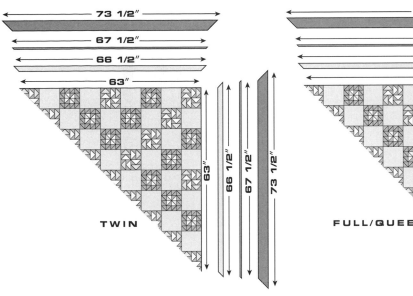

Finishing

1. Complete actual-size quarter pattern for quilting motif, referring to "Plain Block" diagram for orientation of all four quarter blocks.

2. Mark quilting motif on each plain block.

3. Prepare batting and backing.

4. Assemble quilt layers.

5. Quilt plain blocks on marked lines and ¼″ inside seam lines. Quilt in-the-ditch on all seams of pieced blocks and on inner and outer seams of second border.

6. Trim batting and backing to ½″ beyond outermost seam line.

7. Bind quilt edges.

PLAIN BLOCK

ACTUAL-SIZE QUARTER-PATTERN FOR QUILTING MOTIF

Achange of color can give the Dutchman's Puzzle/Yankee Puzzle a completely different feeling. You might want to use colors with more contrast, or make the two blocks very different from one another. You might also consider shading the color values from the center of the quilt out, or from one corner to another, to emphasize the diagonal arrangement of the blocks.

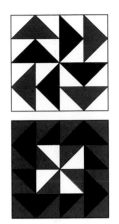

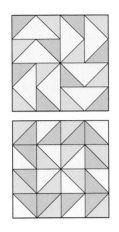

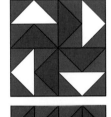

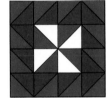
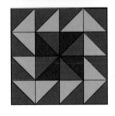

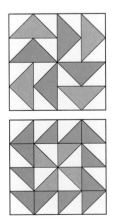
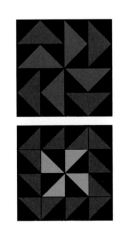
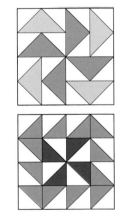

Photocopy this page, then create your own color scheme using colored pencils or markers. Refer to the examples on the previous pages, or design a unique color arrangement to match your decor or please your fancy.

Iff you vary the setting angle from straight to diagonal, use or omit setting squares, or add sashing, you can create many intriguing allover patterns from the Dutchman's Puzzle/Yankee Puzzle blocks. You can also use either of the blocks on its own. These variations may change the size of the quilt; you could compensate by using more or fewer blocks or borders. Diagonal sets may require half- or quarter-blocks.

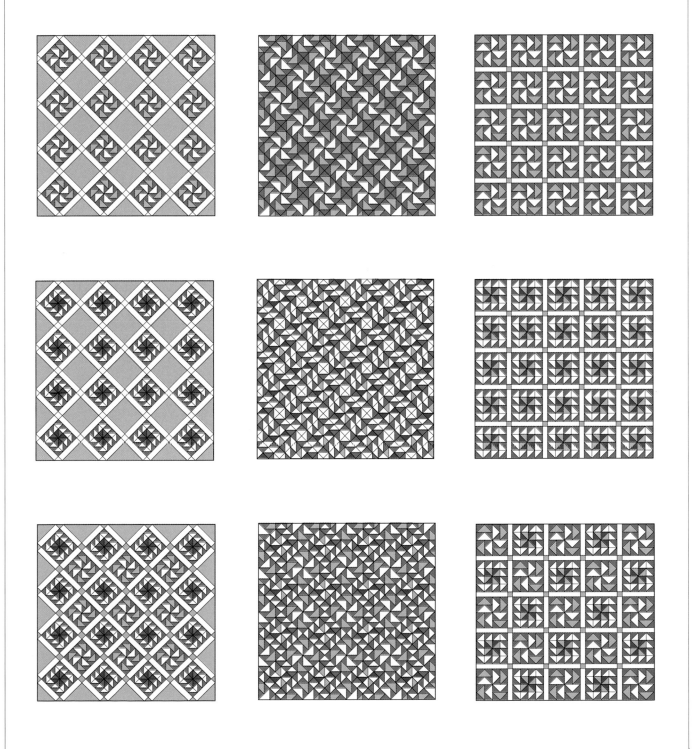

Starry Path Pillow

BY SHARON WREN

Here the traditional Starry Path block is paired with an original clipper ship design, which was pieced to accompany the multicolored star and simply quilted to finish the red one. Note the illusion of intertwined triangles which emerges when each point of the star is a different color.

Note: All dimensions are finished size.

STARRY PATH BLOCK
One block, 10″ square

BOAT BLOCK
4 blocks, 2″ square

FIRST BORDER
4 pieced strips, 2″ wide, cut to size

SECOND BORDER
4 strips, 1″ wide, cut to size
(side pieces added before top and
bottom pieces)

*Note: To make the red-and-blue variation,
see the GREAT IDEA on page 23.*

Yardages are based on 44" fabric. Prepare templates for Starry Path block, referring to drafting schematic, *below*, or actual-size patterns on page 96; prepare templates for Boat block, if desired, using actual-size block pattern, *below*. Cut strips and patches following chart (see "Using the Cutting Charts," page 91). Except for drafting schematic, which gives finished sizes, all dimensions include ¼" seam allowance and strips include extra length, unless otherwise stated.

DIMENSIONS

FINISHED STARRY PATH BLOCK

10" square, about 14⅛" diagonal

FINISHED BOAT BLOCK

2" square, about 2⅞" diagonal

FINISHED PILLOW

16" square

MATERIALS

♦ **RED PRINT**
¼ yd.

♦ **BLUE PRINT**
¼ yd.

♦ **OLIVE PRINT**
¼ yd.

♦ **WHITE PRINT**
½ yd.

♦ **BLUE FLORAL**
¼ yd.

♦ **BLUE SOLID**
¼ yd.

♦ **BACKING** *
½ yd.

♦ **PILLOW BACK**
½ yd.

♦ **BATTING** *

♦ **FIBERFILL FOR STUFFING**

♦ **THREAD**

*Backing and batting should be cut and pieced as necessary so they are at least 4" larger than quilt top on all sides, then trimmed to size after quilting.

DRAFTING SCHEMATIC

(No seam allowance added)

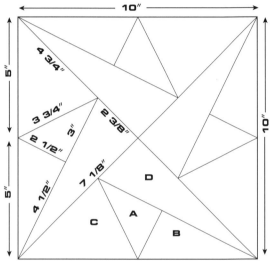

STARRY PATH BLOCK

ACTUAL-SIZE PATTERN

(No seam allowance added)

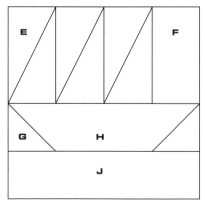

BOAT BLOCK

	FIRST CUT		SECOND CUT		
			Number of Pieces		
Fabric and Yardage	Number of Pieces	Size	For One Starry Path Block	For 4 Boat Blocks	Shape
PLAIN PATCHES					
Blue Floral[1]	–	–	1	–	A
	–	–	1	–	D
	1	1⅞″ × 8″	–	4	E
Blue Print[1]	–	–	1	–	A
	–	–	1	–	D
	1	1⅞″ × 8″	–	4	E
Olive Print[1]	–	–	1	–	A
	–	–	1	–	D
	1	1⅞″ × 8″	–	4	E
Red Print ¼ yd.	–	–	1	–	A
	–	–	1	–	D
	1	1″ × 16″	–	4	H
Blue Solid ¼ yd.	1	1″ × 16″	–	4	J
White Print ½ yd.	1	3⅜″ × 15″	4	–	B
	1	4¼″ × 25″	4	–	C
	1	1⅞″ × 20″	–	12	E
	1	1½″ × 8″	–	4	F
	1	1⅜″ × 8″	–	8	G

[1] Use remainder of fabric from border strips.

CUTTING SCHEMATICS
(Seam allowance included)

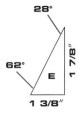

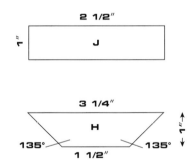

	FIRST CUT		SECOND CUT	
Fabric and Yardage	Number of Pieces	Size	Number of Pieces	Size
FIRST BORDER				
Olive Print[1] ¼ yd.	2	1½″ × 24″	4	1½″ × 12″
Blue Print[1] ¼ yd.	2	1½″ × 24″	4	1½″ × 12″
SECOND BORDER				
Blue Floral[1] ¼ yd.	1	1½″ × 32″	2	1½″ × 16″
	1	1½″ × 36″	2	1½″ × 18″

[1] Reserve remainder of fabric for plain patches.

Starry Path Block

COLOR KEY
- ☐ White print
- ☐ Red print
- ☐ Olive print
- ☐ Blue floral
- ☐ Blue print
- ☐ Blue solid

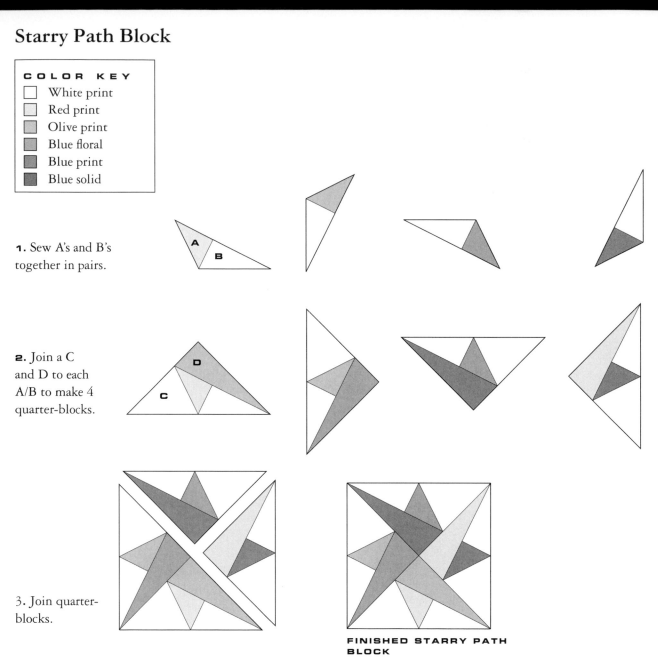

1. Sew A's and B's together in pairs.

2. Join a C and D to each A/B to make 4 quarter-blocks.

3. Join quarter-blocks.

FINISHED STARRY PATH BLOCK

Boat Block

Directions are given below for making one block. Amounts for making all 4 blocks at the same time are in parentheses.

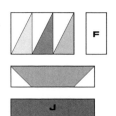

FINISHED BOAT BLOCK

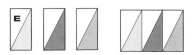

1. Join E's in pairs to make 3 (12) sail rectangles. Join rectangles.

2. Sew G's to H to make one (4) boat bottom.

3. Arrange pieced and plain units in rows as shown. Join rows.

Borders

1. Join strips for first border in pairs. Trim pieced strips to same length as sides of Starry Path block.

2. Sew Boat blocks to ends of 2 pieced strips.

3. Join borders to Starry Path block, short strips at sides and then longer strips at top and bottom.

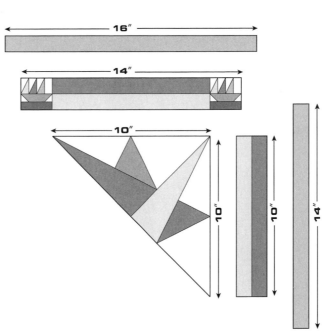

Finishing

1. Prepare batting and backing.
2. Assemble layers for quilting.
3. Quilt in-the-ditch on all seams.
4. Trim batting and backing even with pillow front. Cut pillow back same size.
5. Stitch pillow front and back together, leaving an opening in one side for turning and stuffing. Turn pillow right side out.
6. Stuff pillow. Slipstitch opening closed.

GREAT IDEA

You can give the **Starry Path** block a bold new look just by changing the colors. To make the red-and-blue variation, cut all **A**s, **D**s, and the second border from red print fabric. Cut all **B**s and **C**s from blue print. Cut strips for the first border from white print and blue floral.

To make super-easy **Boat** blocks, cut four 2 1/2" squares from white print fabric (seam allowance included) and quilt the boats instead of piecing them, using the actual-size pattern on page 20.

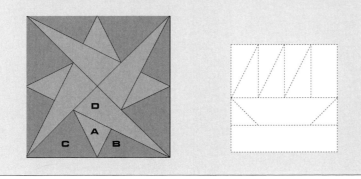

These pillows look very different as the number of colors increases or the background shifts from dark to light. They're good scrap projects, so check the contents of your stash, considering how the scale of different prints will alter the design.

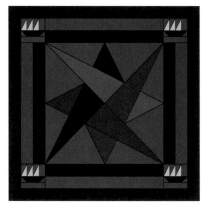

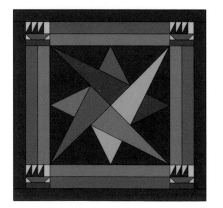

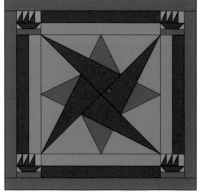

Photocopy this page, then create your own color scheme using colored pencils or markers.

Pine Burr Quilt

Just one quilt block and two colors assembled in a positive/negative pattern make this quilt an easily achieved tour de force. Areas of light color seem to come forward, areas of dark color seem to recede, and different geometric configurations emerge as you adjust your focus. Interestingly, where the corners of four blocks come together, the pattern known as Old Maid's Ramble can be seen.

*Note: All dimensions except for binding are finished size.
Amounts for full/queen are given in parentheses.*

POSITIVE BLOCK
28 (45) blocks, 10″ square

NEGATIVE BLOCK
28 (45) blocks, 10″ square

BINDING
1½″-wide strip, pieced as
necessary and cut to size

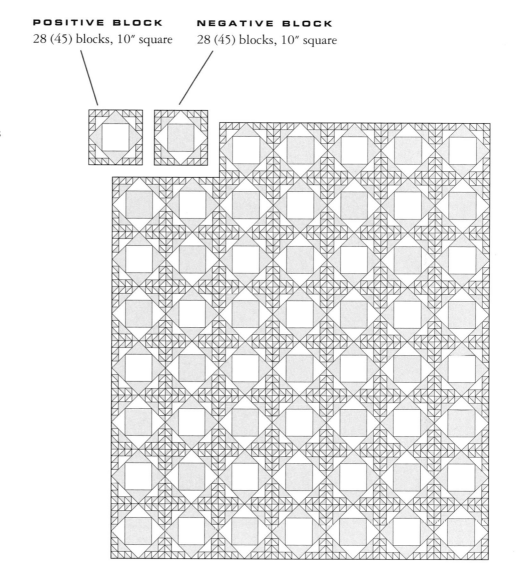

Note: Sizes and amounts for full/queen are given in parentheses.

Yardages are based on 44″ fabric. Prepare templates, if desired, referring to drafting schematic. Cut strips and patches following schematics and chart (see "Using the Cutting Chart," page 91). Except for drafting schematic, which gives finished sizes, all dimensions include ¼″ seam allowance and strips include extra length, unless otherwise stated. (NOTE: Angles on all patches in this project are either 45° or 90°.)

DIMENSIONS

FINISHED BLOCK

10″ square, about 14⅛″ diagonal

FINISHED QUILT

70″ × 80″ (90″ × 100″)

MATERIALS

- ◆ **YELLOW SOLID**
  6½ (8½) yds.

- ◆ **DK. GREEN SOLID**
  6½ (8½) yds.

- ◆ **BACKING** *
  5 (9) yds.

- ◆ **BATTING** *

- ◆ **THREAD**

- ◆ **BINDING**
  Use ½ yd. green solid to make a 1½″ × 340″ (1½″ × 420″) strip.

*Backing and batting should be cut and pieced as necessary so they are at least 4″ larger than quilt top on all sides, then trimmed to size after quilting.

DRAFTING SCHEMATIC

(No seam allowance added)

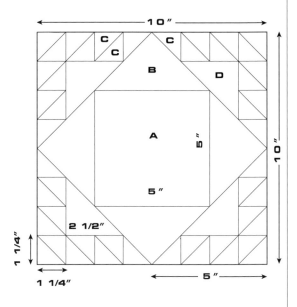

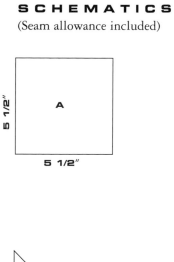

FIRST CUT			SECOND CUT		
			Number of Pieces		
Fabric and Yardage	Number of Pieces	Size	For 28 (45) Positive Blocks	For 28 (45) Negative Blocks	Shape
PLAIN PATCHES					
Yellow Solid 4 (5) yds.	5 (8)	5½" × 40"	28 (45)	–	A
	7 (10)	4⅜" × 40"	–	112 (180)	B
	7 (10)	2⅛" × 40"	224 (360)	–	C
	5 (9)	3⅜" × 40"	112 (180)	–	D
Dk. Green Solid 4 (5) yds.	5 (8)	5½" × 40"	–	28 (45)	A
	7 (10)	4⅜" × 40"	112 (180)	–	B
	7 (10)	2⅛" × 40"	–	224 (360)	C
	5 (9)	3⅜" × 40"	–	112 (180)	D
SPEEDY TRIANGLE SQUARES[1]					
Yellow Solid and Dk. Green Solid 2½ (3½) yds. each	9 (14)	18" sq.	560 (900)	560 (900)	C/C

[1] See Speedy Triangle Squares (page 93). Mark 8 × 8 grids of 2⅛" squares.

5 1/2" (side)
5 1/2" (bottom)
A

4 3/8" (side)
4 3/8" (bottom)
B

2 1/8" (side)
2 1/8" (bottom)
C

3 3/8" (side)
3 3/8" (bottom)
D

GREAT SIZING TIP

Because this pattern will repeat continuously no matter how many blocks are placed in each row or column, you can plan your quilt to be almost any size you wish. Just remember that the length of each edge will be a multiple of 10" (one block). Some examples:

9 blocks in a 3 × 3 layout = 30"-square wallhanging

16 blocks in a 4 × 4 layout = 40"-square wallhanging

24 blocks in a 4 × 6 layout = 40" × 60" crib quilt

The size of this coverlet can be adjusted easily from twin to full/queen if the number of bocks is increased to make two additional rows and columns. Refer to the cutting chart, page 29, for the number of pieces to cut for the different sizes.

TWIN
56 blocks in a 7 × 8 layout

FULL/QUEEN
90 blocks in a 9 × 10 layout

COLOR KEY
☐ Yellow Solid
☐ Dk. green solid

Positive Block

Directions are given below for making one positive block. Amounts for making all 28 (twin) or 45 (full/queen) positive blocks at the same time are given in parentheses. Reverse fabric colors to make the same number of negative blocks.

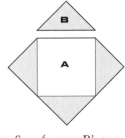

1. Sew 4 green B's to a yellow A to make one (28) (45) center square.

2. Join a C and 2 C/C squares to make one (112) (180) short strip.

3. Join a C and 3 C/C squares to make one (112) (180) long strip.

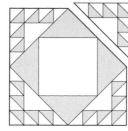

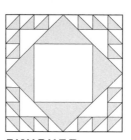

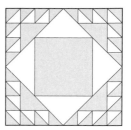

4. Sew short and long strips to a D to make 4 (112) (180) corner triangles.

5. Join units as shown.

FINISHED POSITIVE BLOCK

FINISHED NEGATIVE BLOCK

Quilt Top

Arrange blocks as shown, alternating positive and negative blocks. Join blocks to make rows. Join rows.

TWIN

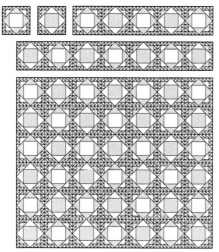

FULL/QUEEN

Finishing

1. Mark quilting design on each A square on quilt top, spacing pairs of lines 1⅜″ apart.

2. Prepare batting and backing.

3. Assemble quilt layers.

4. Quilt on marked design lines and in-the-ditch on all seams.

5. Trim batting and backing to ½″ beyond outermost seam line.

6. Bind quilt edges.

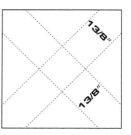

This pattern will look very different if you work with more than two colors. You might decide to make all the blocks the same, or make them all different. If you plan very carefully, you can use color to create the effect of a larger square or diamond within the overall scheme. If you do so, the four corners of a single block may be different colors.

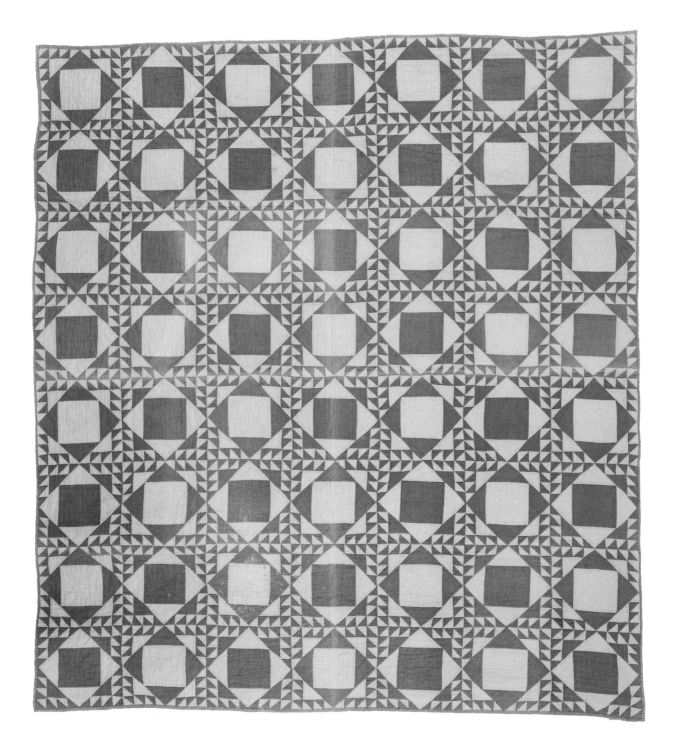

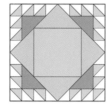

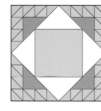

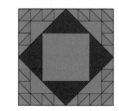
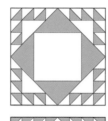

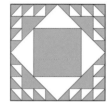
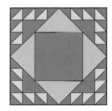

P hotocopy this page, then create your own color scheme using colored pencils or markers. Refer to the examples on the previous page, or design a unique color arrangement to match your decor or please your fancy.

While the arrangement of the Pine Burr block featured here gives an allover pattern that is full of movement, it can be just as appealing when set in other ways. If you add sashing or plain patches between the blocks, the size of the quilt may change; you could compensate by using more or fewer blocks or adding borders.

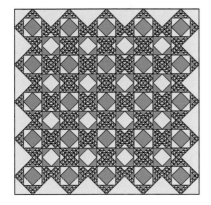
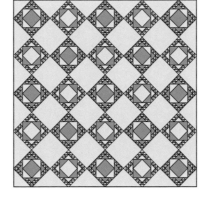
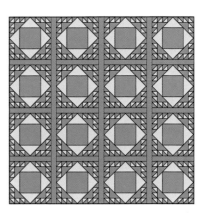

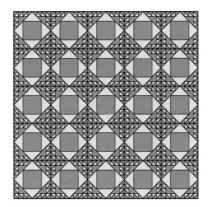
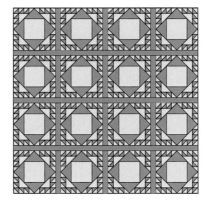

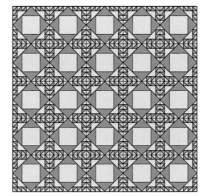
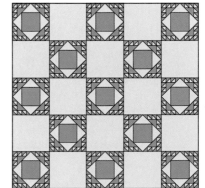

Triangles-in-Triangles Runner

BY JEAN HOBLITZELL

The traditional Economy Patch block, with the center composed of triangles, is the basis of this easy-to-make runner. Jean Hoblitzell is an architect, and her interest in light and space carries over to her quilted pieces. She often uses lightweight upholstery fabrics, chintz, and basketweave textures in her work, and suggests using sturdy interfacing rather than batting to fill a runner, so that it will be crisp and lie flat on the table.

Note: All dimensions are finished size.

CORNER TRIANGLE
4 corner triangles, 4″ on two sides,
5¾″ on third side

BLOCK
4 blocks, 5¾″ square

FIRST BORDER
4 strips, ½″ wide, cut to size
(top and bottom pieces added
before side pieces)

SETTING TRIANGLE
6 setting triangles, 5¾″ on two
sides, 8″ on third side

SECOND BORDER
4 strips, 2″ wide, cut to size

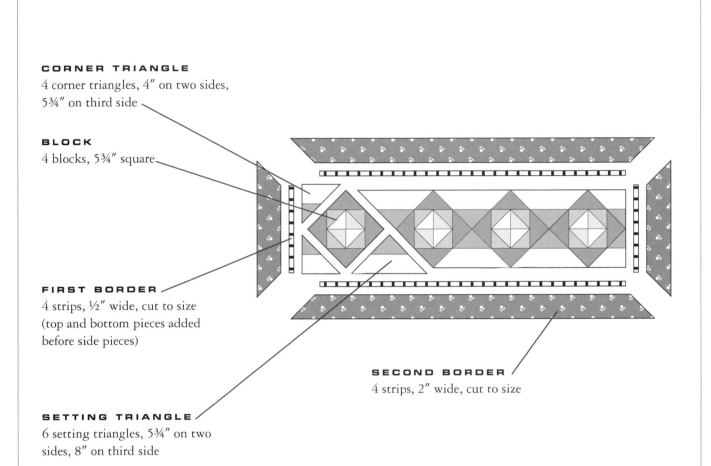

Yardages are based on 44″ fabric. Prepare template, if desired, referring to drafting schematics. Cut strips and patches following schematics and chart (see "Using the Cutting Charts," page 91). Except for drafting schematics, which give finished sizes, all dimensions include ¼″ seam allowance and strips include extra length, unless otherwise stated. (NOTE: Unmarked angles on cutting schematics are either 45° or 90°.)

DIMENSIONS

FINISHED BLOCK

5¾″ square, about 8⅛″ diagonal

FINISHED TABLE RUNNER

13″ × 37″

MATERIALS

- ◆ ANTIQUE WHITE SOLID
  ½ yd.

- ◆ YELLOW SOLID
  ¼ yd.

- ◆ BLUE SOLID
  ¼ yd.

- ◆ GREEN SOLID
  ¼ yd.

- ◆ ORANGE-ON-WHITE PRINT
  ¼ yd.

- ◆ BLACK/WHITE STRIPED
  ¼ yd.

- ◆ BLUE FLORAL
  ¼ yd.

- ◆ BACKING *
  1¼ yds.

- ◆ BATTING *

- ◆ THREAD

*Backing and batting should be cut and pieced as necessary so they are at least 4″ larger than quilt top on all sides, then trimmed to size after quilting.

DRAFTING SCHEMATICS

(No seam allowance added)

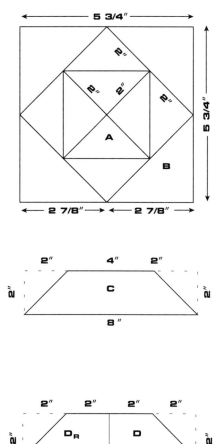

CUTTING SCHEMATICS

(Seam allowance included)

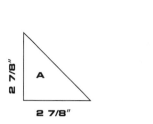

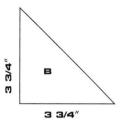

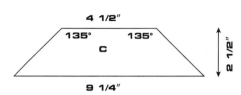

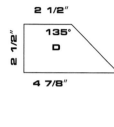

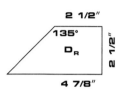

| Fabric and Yardage | FIRST CUT | | SECOND CUT | | | Shape |
| | Number of Pieces | Size | Number of Pieces | | | |
			For 4 Blocks	For 6 Setting Triangles	For 4 Corner Triangles	
PLAIN PATCHES						
Yellow Solid ¼ yd.	1	2⅞" × 40"	8	–	–	A
Orange-on-White Print ¼ yd.	1	2⅞" × 40"	8	–	–	A
Blue Solid ¼ yd.	1	2⅞" × 15"	–	–	4	A[1]
	1	6¼" × 40"	–	6	–	B[1]
Green Solid ¼ yd.	1	6¼" × 40"	16	–	–	B
Antique White Solid ½ yd.	2	2⅞" × 40"	–	–	4	A
	2	2½" × 40"	–	6	–	C
	1	2½" × 40"	–	–	2	D[2]
					2	D_R[2]
FIRST BORDER						
Black/White Striped ¼ yd.	2	1" × 20"				
	2	1" × 40"				
SECOND BORDER						
Blue Floral ¼ yd.	2	2½" × 20"				
	2	2½" × 40"				

[1] Cut blue A's from remainder of strip for B's.
[2] Cut D's and D_R's from same strip.

Block

Directions are given below for making one block. Amounts for making all 4 blocks at the same time are given in parentheses.

1. Join yellow and orange-on-white print A's in pairs to make 2 (8) A/A squares.

2. Join yellow and antique white A's in pairs to make 2 (8) A/A squares.

3. Join 4 A/A's to make one (4) center square.

4. Sew green B's to center square.

FINISHED BLOCK

Table Runner Center

1. Join C's and blue B's in pairs to make 6 setting triangles.

2. Join D's and blue A's in pairs to make 2 corner triangles.

3. Join D_R's and blue A's to make 2 reversed corner triangles.

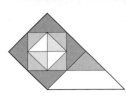
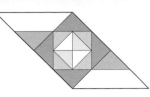

4. Sew one setting triangle each to 2 blocks.

5. Sew 2 setting triangles each to remaining 2 blocks.

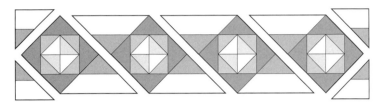

6. Arrange units as shown. Join units.

Borders

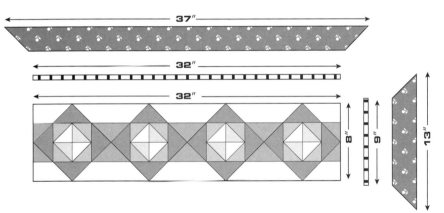

1. Join first border to quilt center, long strips at top and bottom, and then shorter strips at sides.

2. Join second border to first border, mitering corners.

Finishing

1. Prepare batting and backing.

2. Assemble quilt layers.

3. Quilt in-the-ditch on inner edge of first border and around blocks.

4. Bind quilt edges by pressing under edges of quilt top and backing, aligning folds and slipstitching together.

Notice how different parts of this pattern assume prominence or recede when the color values are differently arranged. Experiment with more or fewer colors, as suits your decor or dinnerware, or plan your runner to complement the season.

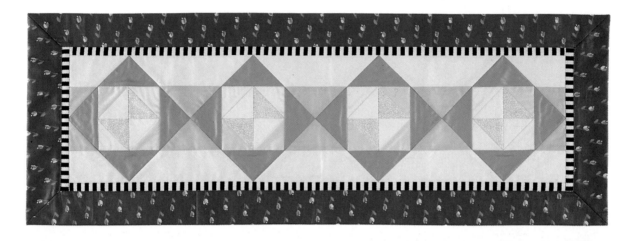

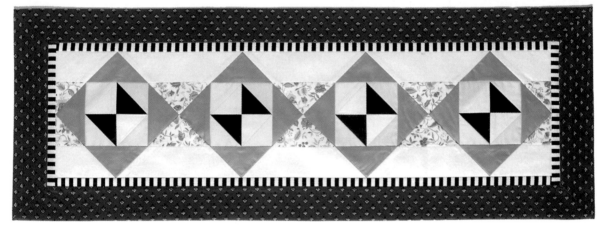

GREAT IDEA

To make a very easy crib quilt or wall-hanging, cut and piece 3 (or 4) strips of blocks, sew them together along the long edges, and then add borders. Your finished piece will be 37" wide × 28" long (or 37" square).

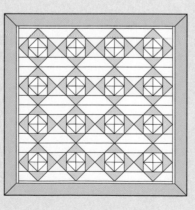

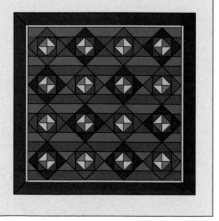

Photocopy this drawing, then create your own color scheme using colored pencils or markers.

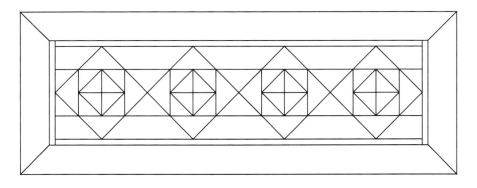

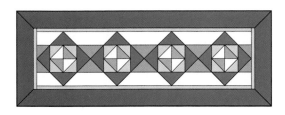 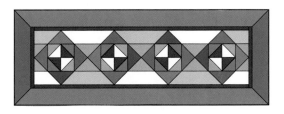

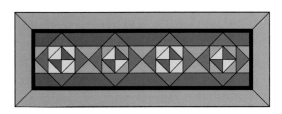 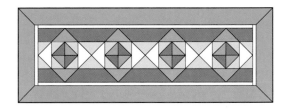

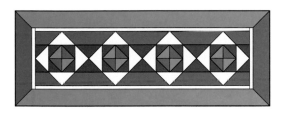 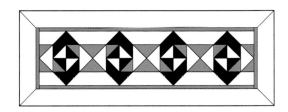

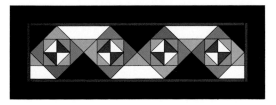 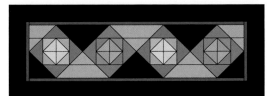

Shoemaker's Puzzle Quilt

T his unusual pattern is a wonderful example of geometry fooling the eye. The block is pieced from just three triangular shapes, and you have only to stand back a short distance to see shifting curves where there are only straight lines. The fabrics in this antique are lovely. Those on the quilt top have curving sprays of leaves and flowers; the backing is a pink and yellow shirting with large polka dots.

Note: Dimensions are finished size.
Amounts for full/queen are given in parentheses.

BLOCK
20 (40) blocks, 15″ square

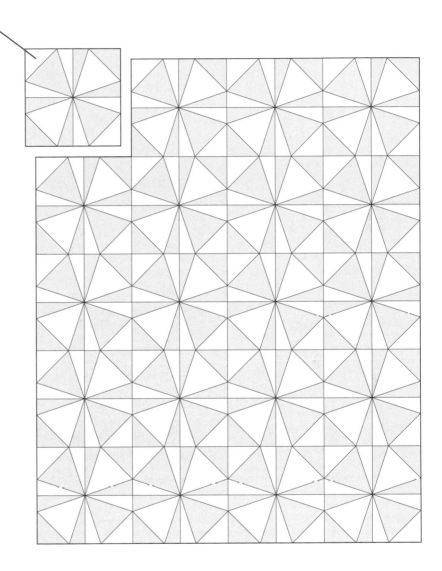

Note: Sizes and amounts for full/queen are given in parentheses.

Yardages are based on 44″ fabric. Prepare templates, if desired, referring to drafting schematics, *below*, or actual-size patterns on pages 94-95. Cut strips and patches following schematics and chart (see "Using the Cutting Charts," page 91). Except for drafting schematic, which gives finished sizes, all dimensions include ¼″ seam allowance and strips include extra length, unless otherwise stated. (NOTE: Unmarked angles on cutting schematics are either 45° or 90°.)

DIMENSIONS

FINISHED BLOCK
15″ square, about 21¼″ diagonal

FINISHED QUILT
60″ × 75″ (90″ × 105″)

MATERIALS

♦ **MUSLIN PRINT**
  3½ (6) yds.

♦ **BROWN PRINT**
  3½ (6) yds.

♦ **BACKING** *
  5 (9) yds.

♦ **BATTING** *

♦ **THREAD**

*Backing and batting should be cut and pieced as necessary so they are at least 4″ larger than quilt top on all sides, then trimmed to size after quilting.

DRAFTING SCHEMATIC
(No seam allowance added)

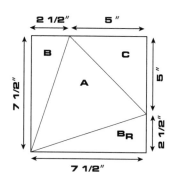

GREAT DESIGN IDEA

You can have a lot of fun playing with the illusion of curves and motion in this simple pattern. Before you purchase your fabric, turn to Changing Colors, pages 51-53, to see some of the possibilities. Use the line drawing to experiment with the different effects you can create by isolating a color in one part of the quilt, or inserting a contrasting color at unexpected intervals. If you are feeling adventurous, think of using a striped fabric.

FIRST CUT			SECOND CUT	
Fabric and Yardage	Number of Pieces	Size	Number of Pieces	Shape
PLAIN PATCHES				
Muslin Print 3½ (6) yds.	6 (12)	7⅞″ × 40″	40 (84)	A
	10 (21)	3⅛″ × 40″	40 (84)	B
			40 (84)	B_R[1]
	3 (6)	5⅞″ × 40″	40 (84)	C
Brown Print 3½ (6) yds.	6 (12)	7⅞″ × 40″	40 (84)	A
	10 (21)	3⅛″ × 40″	40 (84)	B
			40 (84)	B_R[1]
	3 (6)	5⅞″ × 40″	40 (84)	C

[1] No extra strips required. Cut reversed patches from same strips as B's.

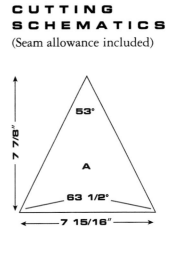

53°

7 7/8″

A

63 1/2°

7 15/16″

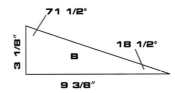

71 1/2°

3 1/8″

B

18 1/2°

9 3/8″

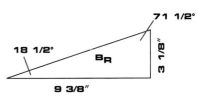

71 1/2°

18 1/2°

B_R

3 1/8″

9 3/8″

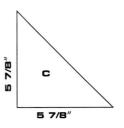

5 7/8″

C

5 7/8″

The size of this coverlet can be adjusted easily from twin to full/queen if the number of blocks is increased to make two additional rows and columns. Refer to the cutting chart, page 47, for the number of pieces to cut for the different sizes.

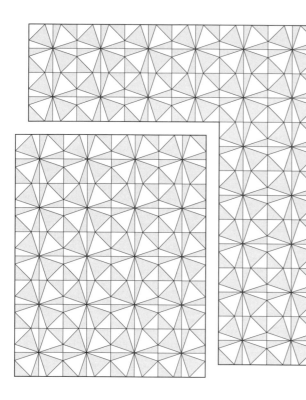

TWIN
20 blocks in a 4 × 5 layout

FULL/QUEEN
42 blocks in a 6 × 7 layout

GREAT SIZING TIP

Because this pattern will repeat continuously no matter how many blocks are placed in each row or column, you can plan your quilt to be almost any size you wish. Just remember that the length of each edge will be a multiple of 15" (one block). Some examples:

1 block = an easy-to-make pillow
9 blocks in a 3 × 3 layout = 45" × 45" wallhanging
12 blocks in a 3 × 4 layout = 45" × 60" quilt
16 blocks in a 4 × 4 layout = 60" × 60" quilt
30 blocks in a 5 × 6 layout = 75" × 90" quilt

4-Patch Block

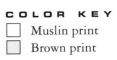
Directions are given below for making one 4-patch block. Amounts for making all 20 blocks (twin) or 42 blocks (full/queen) at the same time are given in parentheses.

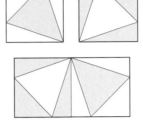

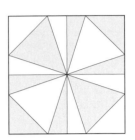

1. Sew a muslin B, B_R, and C to a brown A, to make a positive quarter-block. Make 2 (40) (84).

2. Sew a brown B, B_R, and C to a muslin A, to make a negative quarter-block. Make 2 (40) (84).

3. Join quarter-blocks, alternating colors and rotating as shown.

FINISHED BLOCK

Quilt Top

Arrange blocks as shown. Join blocks to make rows. Join rows.

TWIN

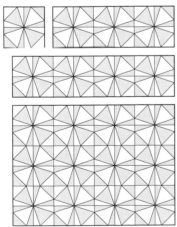

FULL/QUEEN

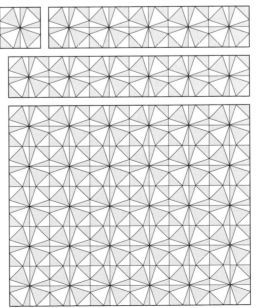

Finishing

1. Mark allover quilting design on backing. Mark a grid of 6″ × 11″ rectangles on the diagonal.

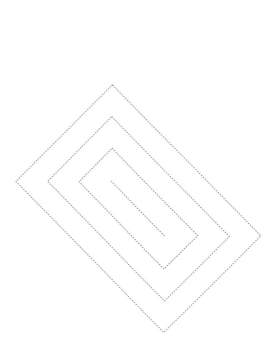

2. Mark lines 1″ apart for inward echo quilting in each rectangle.

3. Prepare batting and backing, allowing extra at each side of backing for making self-binding.

4. Assemble quilt layers.

5. Quilt on marked design lines.

6. Trim backing to size and fold it over quilt top to make ¼″-wide self-binding with butted corners.

Y ou can choose different colors to alter the mood of this pattern as you would for any quilt, but you might also like to emphasize the effect of allover movement by shading the color values from the center of the quilt out, or from one corner to another. If you make all of the blocks in your quilt either all positive or all negative it will seem to be another pattern altogether. Note what happens when you add a third or fourth color to the block.

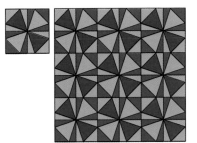

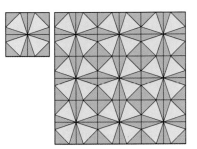

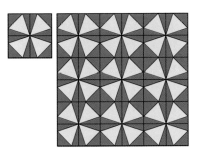

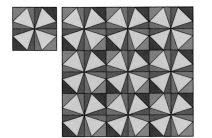

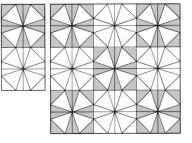

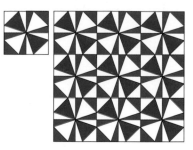
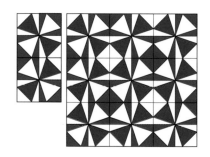

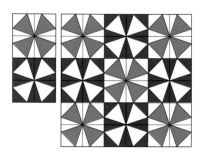
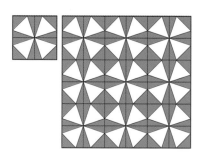
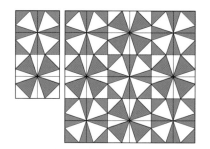
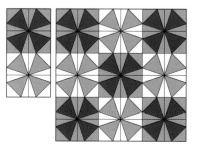
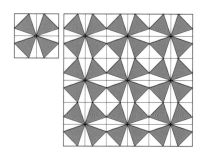
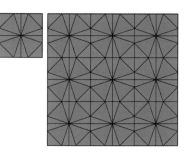
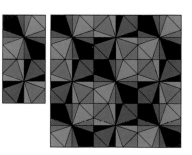

Photocopy this page, then create your own color scheme using colored pencils or markers. Refer to the examples on the previous pages, or design a unique color arrangement to match your decor or please your fancy.

Baskets Quilt

A bold sawtooth border gives a lively balance to this rendition of the always-popular basket pattern. Turn to the photo on page 62 and you'll see that the quilter of this antique piece attached her borders in a rather eccentric manner; we have given instructions for a symmetrical arrangement.

*Note: All dimensions except for binding are finished size.
Amounts for full/queen are given in parentheses.*

BLOCK
13 blocks, 10″ square, with appliquéd handles

CORNER TRIANGLE
4 corner triangles, 7″ on two sides, about 10″ on third side

SETTING TRIANGLE
8 setting triangles, 10″ on two sides, about 14″ on third side

FIRST BORDER
4 pieced strips, 3½″-wide, plus four plain 3½″ corner squares

SECOND BORDER
4 pieced strips, 3½″-wide, plus four plain 3½″ corner squares

THIRD BORDER
4 pieced strips, 3½″-wide, plus four plain 3½″ corner squares

FOURTH BORDER
2 (4) pieced strips, 3½″-wide (plus four plain 3½″ corner squares)

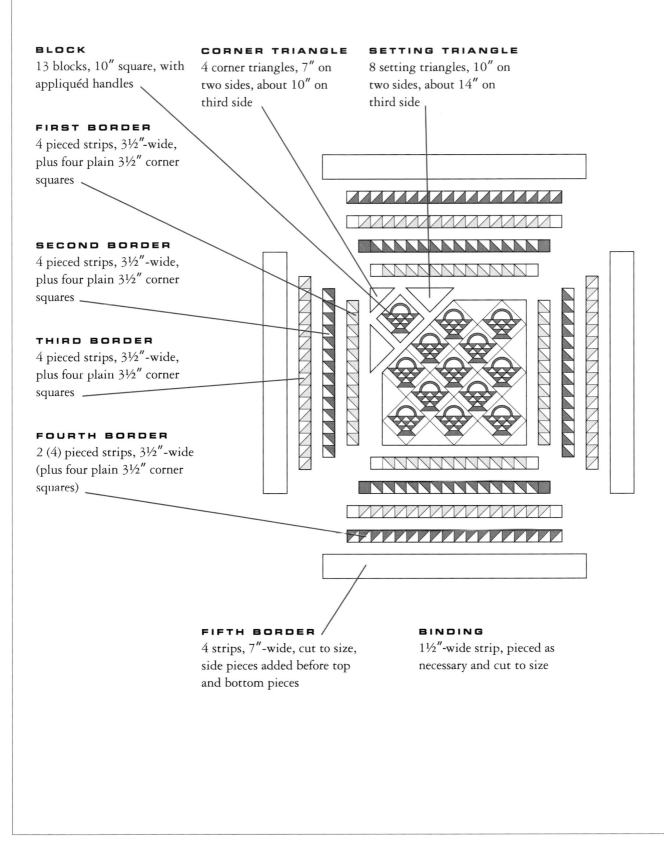

FIFTH BORDER
4 strips, 7″-wide, cut to size, side pieces added before top and bottom pieces

BINDING
1½″-wide strip, pieced as necessary and cut to size

Note: Sizes and amounts for full/queen are given in parentheses.

Yardages are based on 44″ fabric. Prepare templates, if desired, referring to drafting schematics. Cut strips and patches following schematics and chart (see "Using the Cutting Charts," page 91). Cut binding and basket handles as directed below. Except for drafting schematics, which give finished sizes, all dimensions include ¼″ seam allowance. Except for basket handles, all strips include extra length, unless otherwise stated. (NOTE: Unmarked angles on cutting schematics are either 45° or 90°.)

DIMENSIONS

FINISHED BLOCK
10″ square, about 14⅛″ diagonal

FINISHED QUILT
77″ × 84″ (84″ square)

MATERIALS

◆ **MUSLIN SOLID**
9 (9½) yds.

◆ **BLUE DOTTED**
1½ yds.

◆ **BROWN STRIPED**
3½ (4) yds.

◆ **BACKING***
5 (5½) yds.

◆ **BATTING***

◆ **THREAD**

◆ **BINDING**
Use ½ yd. muslin solid to make a 1½″ × 340″ (1½″ × 360″) strip.

◆ **BASKET HANDLES**
Use ½ yd. brown striped to cut 13 bias strips for appliqué, 1¾″ × 20½″.

*Backing and batting should be cut and pieced as necessary so they are at least 4″ larger than quilt top on all sides, then trimmed to size after quilting.

DRAFTING SCHEMATICS
(No seam allowance added)

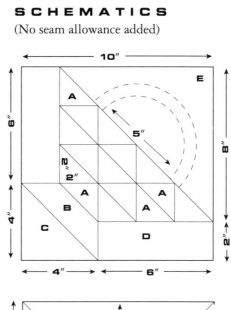

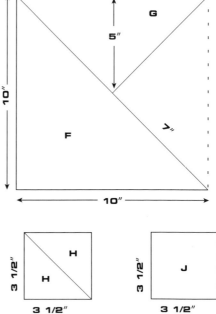

Fabric and Yardage	Number of Pieces	Size	For 13 Blocks	For 8 Setting and 4 Corner Blocks	For First Border	For Second Border	For Third Border	For Fourth Border	Shape
FIRST CUT			**SECOND CUT**						
			Number of Pieces						
PLAIN PATCHES									
Brown Striped ½ yd.	2	2⅞" × 40"	52	–	–	–	–	–	A
	1	4" × 40"	–	–	–	4	–	(4)	J
Muslin Solid 4¾ yds.	2	2½" × 100"	28	–	–	–	–	–	D
	2	8⅞" × 40"	13	–	–	–	–	–	E
	2	10⅞" × 40"	–	8	–	–	–	–	F
	1	7⁹⁄₁₆" × 18"	–	4	–	–	–	–	G
	1	4" × 40"	–	–	4	–	4	–	J
FIFTH BORDER									
	2	7½" × 80"							
	2	7½" × 87" (4½" × 94")							

Fabric and Yardage	Number of Pieces	Size	For 13 Blocks	For First Border	For Second Border	For Third Border	For Fourth Border	Shape
FIRST CUT			**SECOND CUT**					
			Number of Pieces					
SPEEDY TRIANGLE SQUARES[1]								
Brown Striped and Muslin Solid 1¼ (1¾) yds. each	1	15⅜" × 21⅛"	65	–	–	–	–	A/A[2]
	3 (4)	18½" sq.	–	–	56	–	36 (72)	H/H[3]
Blue dotted and Muslin Solid 1¼ yds. each	4	18½" sq.	–	48	–	64	–	H/H[3]
STRIP-PIECED BIAS SQUARES[4]								
Muslin Solid and Brown Striped 1 yd. each	2	2¹⁄₁₆" × 40"						A/B/C
	2	1¹⁵⁄₁₆" × 40"						
	2	3½" × 40"						

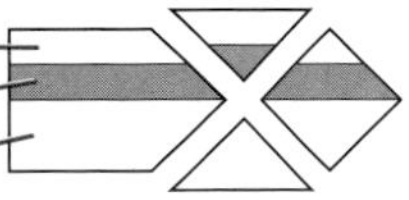

[1] See Speedy Triangle Squares (p. 93).

[2] Mark 5 × 7 grids of 2⅞" squares.

[3] Mark 4 × 4 grids of 4⅜" squares.

[4] Cut strips on the bias and join lengthwise with brown striped between muslin solid strips as shown. Cut 13 A/B/C squares.

CUTTING SCHEMATICS

(Seam allowance included)

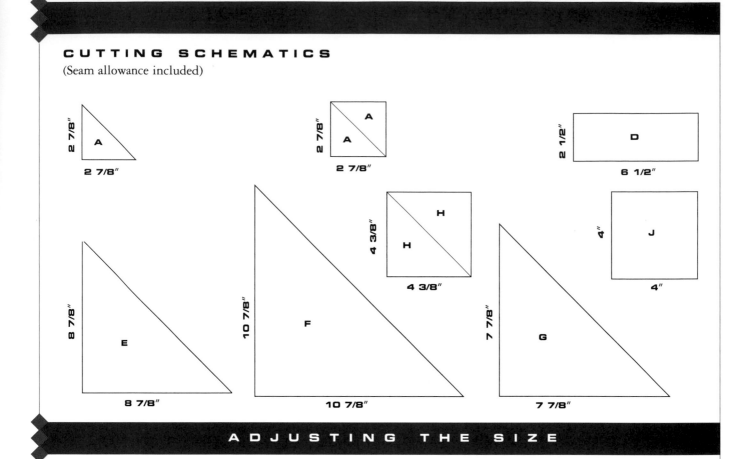

A — 2 7/8" × 2 7/8"

A / A — 2 7/8" × 2 7/8"

D — 2 1/2" × 6 1/2"

E — 8 7/8" × 8 7/8"

F — 10 7/8" × 10 7/8"

H / H — 4 3/8" × 4 3/8"

G — 7 7/8" × 7 7/8"

J — 4" × 4"

ADJUSTING THE SIZE

This quilt can be enlarged easily from twin to full/queen by adjusting the fourth and fifth borders. For the fourth (pieced) border, add plain corner squares to the ends of the top and bottom strips and make two strips for the sides. For the fifth (plain) border, increase the length of the strips to fit.

TWIN

3 pieced strips at sides,
4 pieced strips at top
and bottom

FULL/QUEEN

4 pieced strips on all sides

Block

Directions are given below for making one block. Amounts for making all 13 blocks at the same time are given in parentheses.

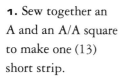

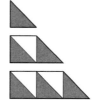

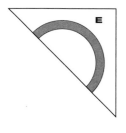

1. Sew together an A and an A/A square to make one (13) short strip.

2. Sew together an A and two A/A squares to make 2 (26) long strips.

3. Arrange pieced and plain units as shown to make 3 rows. Join rows.

4. Join one D to piece from Step 3 and another to remaining long strip.

5. Press under ¼" on long edges of bias strip for handle. Curve strip into a semi-circle and appliqué it on E.

6. Arrange units as shown. Join units.

FINISHED BLOCK

Quilt Center

Arrange units as shown. Join units to make rows. Join rows.

Borders

Varying amounts and directions for full/queen are given in parentheses. Refer to diagrams for orientation of triangle squares in sawtooth strips on all sides of quilt. (Left- and right-side strips are identical; top and bottom strips are identical and the opposite of side strips. Refer to the "Components" diagram on page 55 as well.)

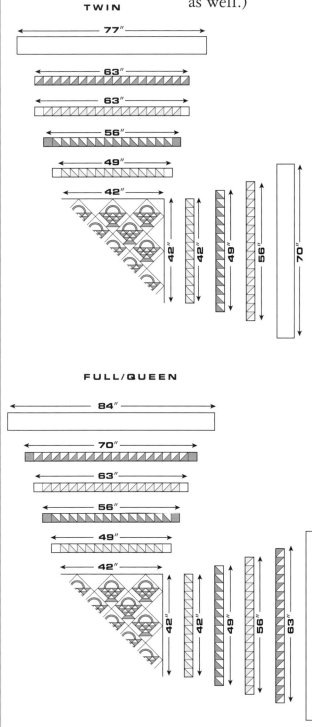

1. For first border, join 12 blue/muslin H/H squares to make 4 sawtooth strips. Sew a muslin J to ends of top and bottom strips.

2. For second border, join 14 brown/muslin H/H squares to make 4 sawtooth strips. Sew a brown J to ends of top and bottom strips.

3. For third border, join 16 blue/muslin H/H squares to make 4 sawtooth strips. Sew a muslin J to ends of top and bottom strips.

4. For fourth border, join 18 brown/muslin H/H squares to make 2 (4) sawtooth strips. (Sew a brown J to ends of top and bottom strips.)

5. Join first, second, and third borders to quilt center, short strips at sides, then longer strips at top and bottom.

6. Join fourth border to quilt top and bottom. (Join short strips to quilt sides, then longer strips to quilt top and bottom.)

7. Join fifth border to quilt, short strips at sides, then longer strips at top and bottom.

Finishing

Amounts for full/queen are given in parentheses.

1. Mark quilting designs on quilt top: Mark lines for single-outline, double-outline, echo, and allover quilting ½″ from seams and/or ½″ apart. Mark 1½″ semi-circles under basket handle. For plain and pieced border squares, mark 2½″ circles. For plain border, mark echoing diamonds, starting at center of each quilt side and working outward to ends; mark 20 diamonds on quilt sides; mark 22 (24) on top and bottom.

2. Prepare batting and backing.

3. Assemble quilt layers.

4. Quilt on marked lines.

5. Trim batting and backing to ½″ beyond outermost seam line.

6. Bind quilt edges.

BASKET BLOCK

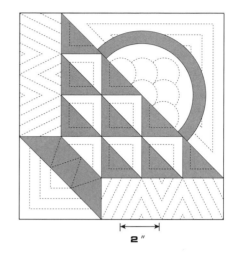

2″

BORDER SQUARE

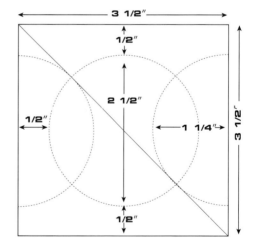

3 1/2″

1/2″

1/2″

2 1/2″

1 1/4″

3 1/2″

1/2″

SETTING TRIANGLE

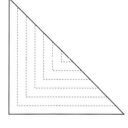

CORNER TRIANGLE

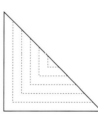

PLAIN BORDER

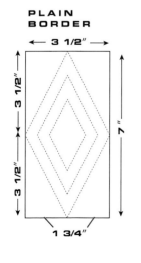

← 3 1/2″ →

3 1/2″

3 1/2″

7″

1 3/4″

TWIN

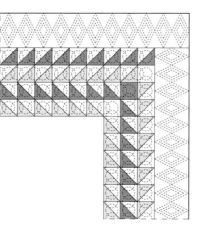

FULL QUEEN

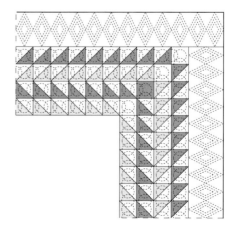

The fewer colors used in a basket quilt, the more sophisticated it is likely to appear. But this pattern easily assumes the mood of the prints and colors from which it is made, so go as bright, funky, nostalgic, or sweet as you wish, and feel free to choose a different color for each basket.

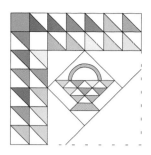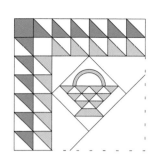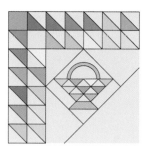

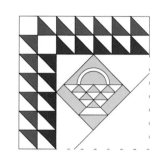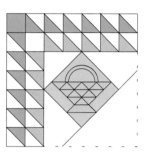

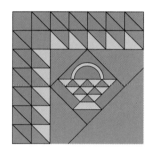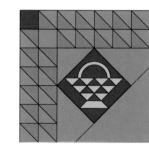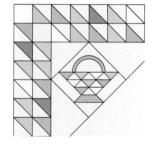

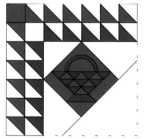

Photocopy this page, then create your own color scheme using colored pencils or markers. Refer to the examples on the previous pages, or design a unique color arrangement to match your decor or please your fancy.

The basket pattern can be very charming set with sashing, or the blocks can be turned to face the edges or the center—a nice touch if you plan to hang the quilt. Adding sashing will change the size of the quilt; use plain borders or plan to recalculate the sawteeth.

GREAT IDEA

Here are two ways you could use the Basket block to make a wallhanging. Note that two strips of white were added to the block to accommodate the flower appliqués.

Winter Storm Warning

BY POLLY WHITEHORN

T his wallhanging was begun in a workshop in which the participants turned and rearranged triangles to achieve different effects. Polly Whitehorn found that her piece had the quality of a wintry landscape. She added freehand machine-stitching to delineate a tree and fence, and used tiny iridescent beads to represent snowflakes. The hanging is quilted in a swirling pattern that evokes the winds.

Note: All dimensions except for binding are finished size.

PLAIN BLOCK
14 blocks, 3″ square

BORDER
4 strips, 2″ wide, cut to size

BINDING
1½″-wide strip, pieced as necessary and cut to size

PIECED BLOCK
16 blocks, 3″ square

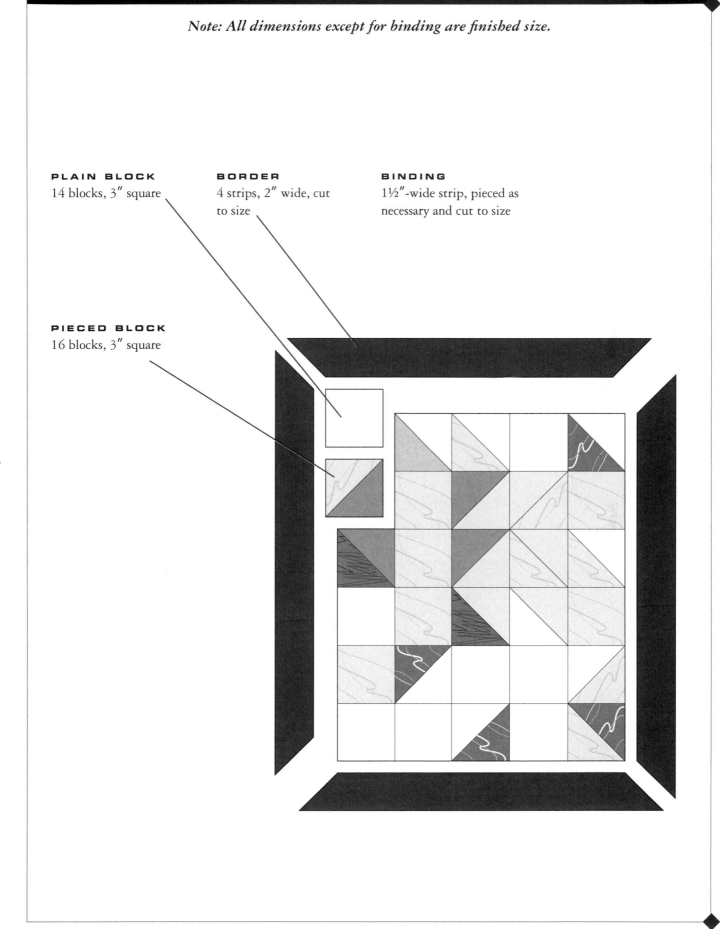

Note: Diagram on page 73 shows quilt one-third of actual size.

Yardages are based on 44″ fabric. Prepare templates, if desired, referring to drafting schematics. Cut strips and patches following schematics and chart (see "Using the Cutting Charts," page 91). Cut binding as directed below. Except for drafting schematics, which give finished sizes, all dimensions include ¼″ seam allowance and strips include extra length, unless otherwise stated. (NOTE: Angles on all patches in this project are either 45° or 90°.)

DIMENSIONS

FINISHED BLOCK
3″ square, about 4¼″ diagonal

FINISHED WALLHANGING
19″ × 22″

MATERIALS

- **WHITE SOLID**
  ¼ yd.
- **LT. GRAY PRINT**
  ¼ yd.
- **LT./DK. PURPLE PRINT**
  ¼ yd.
- **DK. MAUVE SOLID**
  ¼ yd.
- **BROWN/LAVENDER PRINT**
  ¼ yd.
- **LT. BLUE/ LAVENDER PRINT**
  ¼ yd.
- **MAROON PRINT**
  ¼ yd.
- **DK. GRAY SOLID**
  ¾ yd.
- **BACKING** *
  ¾ yd.
- **BATTING** *
- **THREAD**
- **TINY BEADS**
  100 white iridescent
- **BINDING**
  Use ¼ yd. black
  solid to make a
  1½″ × 92″ strip.

*Backing and batting should be cut and pieced as necessary so they are at least 4″ larger than quilt top on all sides, then trimmed to size after quilting.

DRAFTING SCHEMATICS
(No seam allowance added)

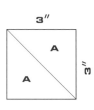

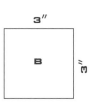

CUTTING SCHEMATICS

(Seam allowance included)

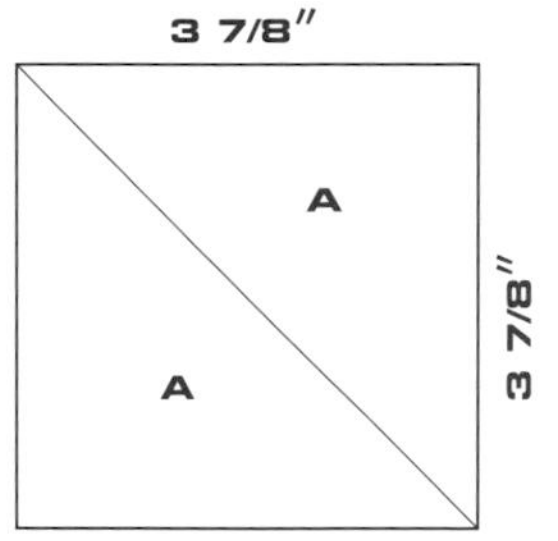

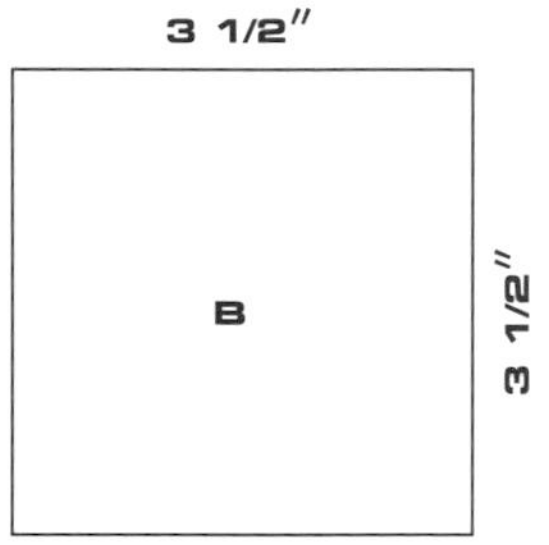

3 7/8"

3 7/8"

A

A

3 1/2"

3 1/2"

B

Fabric and Yardage	FIRST CUT		SECOND CUT	
	Number of Pieces	Size	Number of Pieces	Shape
PLAIN PATCHES				
White ¼ yd.	1	3⅞" × 20"	8	A
	1	3½" × 40"	8	B
Lt. Gray ¼ yd.	1	3⅞" × 20"	6	A
Lt./Dk. Purple ¼ yd.	—	—	1	A
Dk. Mauve ¼ yd.	1	3⅞" × 10"	4	A
Brown/ Lavender ¼ yd.	1	3⅞" × 10"	4	A
Lt. Blue/ Lavender ¼ yd.	1	3⅞" × 20"	7	A
	1	3½" × 40"	6	B
Maroon ¼ yd.	1	3⅞" × 10"	2	A
BORDERS				
Dk. Gray ½ yd.	2	2½" × 29"		
	2	2½" × 32"		

GREAT SIZING TIP

Because this hanging is made from such simple blocks (a plain square and a same-size triangle square) it is very easy to change the size of your hanging by changing the block size. Decide how long you want your hanging to be (less any borders) and divide that dimension by the number of rows in the assembly diagram. The result will be the finished size of the square (the length of the perpendicular legs of the triangle) with which you should work. (Multiply this by the number of columns across the assembly diagram to find the width of your hanging.)

For example, to make a hanging 30" long: 30" divided by 6 rows = 5" squares or triangles; when multiplied by 5 columns, you see that the hanging will be 25" wide. Be sure to add the width of the borders to your final calculations and also to add seam allowance before cutting your pieces.

COLOR KEY

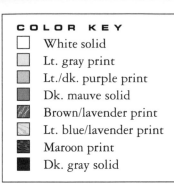

- □ White solid
- ▢ Lt. gray print
- ▨ Lt./dk. purple print
- ▨ Dk. mauve solid
- ◩ Brown/lavender print
- ◪ Lt. blue/lavender print
- ▨ Maroon print
- ■ Dk. gray solid

Pieced Block

Join A's in pairs to make A/A squares as shown in the chart.

NUMBER TO MAKE	COLOR COMBINATION
1	White and lt. gray
1	White and lt./dk. purple
3	White and brown/lavender
3	White and lt. blue/lavender
2	Lt. gray and dk. mauve
1	Lt. gray and maroon
2	Lt. gray and lt. blue/lavender
1	Lt. blue/lavender and dk. mauve
1	Lt. blue/lavender and brown/lavender
1	Dk. mauve and maroon

FINISHED PIECED BLOCK

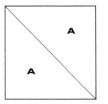

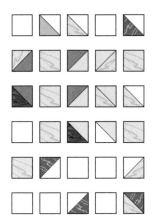

Quilt Center

Arrange pieced and plain blocks as shown. Join blocks to make 6 rows. Join rows.

Border

Join border strips to quilt center, mitering corners.

Finishing

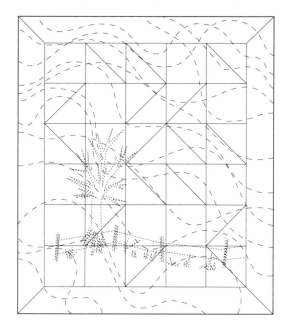

1. If desired, enlarge pattern shown one-third of actual size on page 73. Mark designs on quilt top: Mark tree, fence, and grass on quilt center. Mark swirls of wind on quilt center and border.

2. Make black tree, fence, and grass with free-machine embroidery, straight-stitch hand-embroidery, or indelible fine-point pen.

3. Prepare batting and backing.

4. Assemble layers for quilting.

5. Quilt swirls of wind with white, iridescent blue, and gold metallic threads.

6. Bind quilt edges.

7. Trim batting and backing to ½″ beyond outermost seam line.

8. Sew a sprinkling of bead "snowflakes" all over quilt center, making sure stitches don't go through to back of quilt.

Give yourself time to experiment with the effects of color and layout on design. Follow the directions for our hanging using the palette of your choice: Lay out the pieces, and before you sew any of them together, rearrange them until you are pleased with the effect.

Photocopy this page, then create your own color scheme using colored pencils or markers. Refer to the examples shown, *opposite*, or design a unique color arrangement to match your decor or please your fancy.

Lady of the Lake Quilt

This is a classic pattern with the blocks set on point and rotated so that both the large and small red and white triangles seem to spin, giving the quilt a sense of movement. Pinwheels and hourglasses appear where the corners of the blocks meet. The Rocky Glen quilt folded on the trunk is a variation of this pattern; see page 85 for how to adapt the directions.

Note: All dimensions except for binding are finished size.
Amounts for full/queen are given in parentheses.

DARK HALF-BLOCK
8 (10) half-blocks, 13½″ on two sides, about 19⅛″ on third side

BINDING
1½″-wide strip pieced as necessary and cut to size

WHOLE BLOCK
24 (40) blocks, 13½″ square

LIGHT HALF-BLOCK
8 (10) half-blocks, 13½″ on two sides, about 19⅛″ on third side

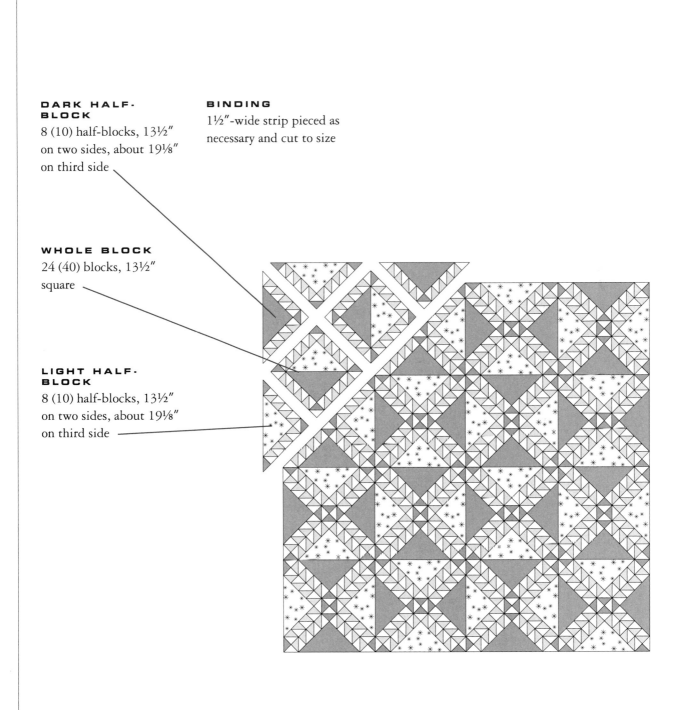

Note: Sizes and amounts for full/queen are given in parentheses.

Yardages are based on 44" fabric. Prepare templates, if desired, referring to drafting schematic. Cut strips and patches following schematics and chart (see "Using the Cutting Charts," page 91). Except for drafting schematic, which gives finished sizes, all dimensions include ¼" seam allowance and strips include extra length, unless otherwise stated. (NOTE: Angles on all patches in this project are either 45° or 90°.)

DIMENSIONS

FINISHED BLOCK
13½" square, about 19⅛" diagonal

FINISHED QUILT
76½" (95⅝") square

MATERIALS

- **MUSLIN SOLID**
  3¼ (4) yds.

- **RED SOLID**
  2½ (4) yds.

- **FOUR (FIVE) TINY RED-ON-EGGSHELL PRINTS**
  1 yd. each

- **EIGHT BROWN AND/OR RED ALLOVER PRINTS**
  1/4 yd. each

- **BACKING** *
  5 (9) yds.

- **BATTING** *

- **THREAD**

- **BINDING**
  Use ½ yd. red solid to make a 1½" × 320" (1½" × 430") strip.

*Backing and batting should be cut and pieced as necessary so they are at least 4" larger than quilt top on all sides, then

DRAFTING SCHEMATIC

(No seam allowance added)

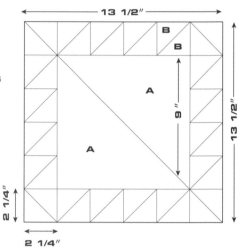

CUTTING SCHEMATICS

(Seam allowance included)

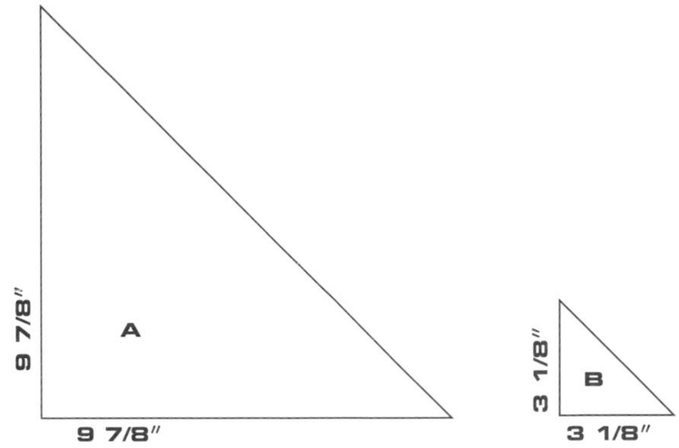

A — 9 7/8" × 9 7/8"

B — 3 1/8" × 3 1/8"

	FIRST CUT		SECOND CUT			
			Number of Pieces			
Fabric and Yardage	**Number of Pieces**	**Size**	For 24 (40) Whole Blocks	For 8 (10) Light Half-Blocks	For 8 (10) Dark Half-Blocks	**Shape**
PLAIN PATCHES						
Red Solid ½ (¾) yd.	1 (2)	9⅞" × 40"	–	8 (10)	–	A
	1 (2)	3⅛" × 40"	–	16 (20)	–	B
Red-on-Eggshell Prints ½ yd. each	4 (5)	9⅞" sq.	–	–	8 (10)	A[1]
Muslin Solid ¼ yd.	1	3⅛" × 40"	–	–	16 (20)	B
SPEEDY TRIANGLE SQUARES[2]						
Red Solid 1 (1¾) yd. and Red-on-Eggshell Prints ½ yd. each	6 (10)	10⅞" × 20¾"	24 (40)	–	–	A/A[3]
Red Solid and Muslin Solid ½ (1) yd. each	2 (3)	16⅝" × 19¾"	96 (160)	8 (10)	8 (10)	B/B[4]
Muslin Solid 1½ (1¾) yds. and Brown/Red Prints ¼ yd. each	8 (14)	13½" × 19¾"	384 (640)	–	–	B/B[5]
	8 (10)	4⅛" × 13½"	–	64 (80)	64 (80)	B/B[6]

[1]Cut strips from 4 (5) different prints.

[2]See Speedy Triangle Squares (page 93).

[3]Mark 1 × 2 grids with 9⅞" squares on 4 (5) different prints.

[4]Mark 5 × 6 grids with 3⅛" squares.

[5]Mark 4 × 6 grids with 3⅛" squares on 8 different prints.

[6]Mark 4 × 6 grids with 3⅛" squares on 8 different prints.

The size of this coverlet can be adjusted easily from twin to full/queen if the number of whole and partial blocks is increased to make two additional center rows. Refer to the cutting chart, *previous page*, for the number of pieces to cut for the different sizes.

TWIN
24 whole blocks,
8 light and 8
dark half-blocks

FULL/QUEEN
40 whole blocks,
10 light and 10
dark half-blocks

GREAT IDEA

You could use four Lady of the Lake blocks, (or four half-blocks), to make a wallhanging. Refer to Changing Colors and Changing Sets, pages 81-84, for some ideas, and use the line drawing to work out a configuration that appeals to you.

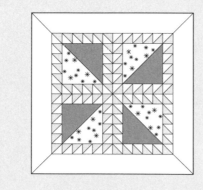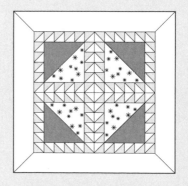

Whole Block

Directions are given below for making one whole block. Amounts for making all 24 (twin) or 40 (full/queen) whole blocks at the same time are given in parentheses.

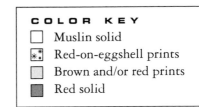

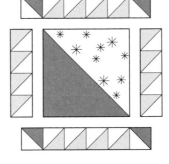

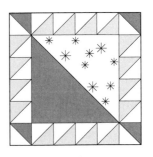

1. Join 4 print-and-solid B/B's and 2 solid B/B's to make 2 (48) (80) long strips.

2. Join 4 print-and-solid B/B's to make 2 (48) (80) short strips.

3. Arrange pieced units as shown. Join to make 3 rows. Join rows.

FINISHED WHOLE BLOCK

Half-block

(Make 8 each of light and dark half-blocks for twin, 10 each for full/queen.) Stitch patches into units following sequence of whole block. Arrange pieced units as shown. Join to make 3 rows. Join rows.

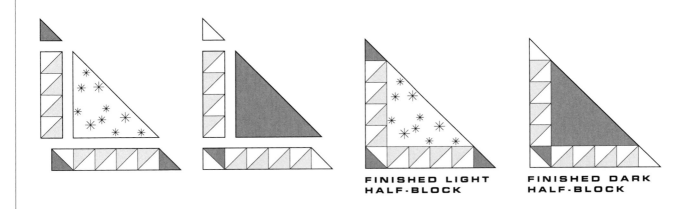

FINISHED LIGHT HALF-BLOCK

FINISHED DARK HALF-BLOCK

Quilt Top

Arrange whole and partial blocks as shown. Join units to make rows. Join rows.

TWIN

FULL/QUEEN

Finishing

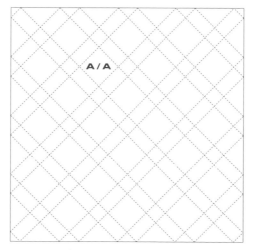

A/A

1. Prepare batting and backing.

2. Assemble quilt layers.

3. Quilt in-the-ditch on seams around all A/A's, extending quilting lines completely across quilt.

4. Trim backing and batting to ½″ beyond outermost seam line.

5. Bind quilt edges.

Whether you use assorted or matching fabrics for your sawtooth strips, make all the corners from two contrasting colors to get the full effect of pinwheels and hourglasses dancing across the surface.

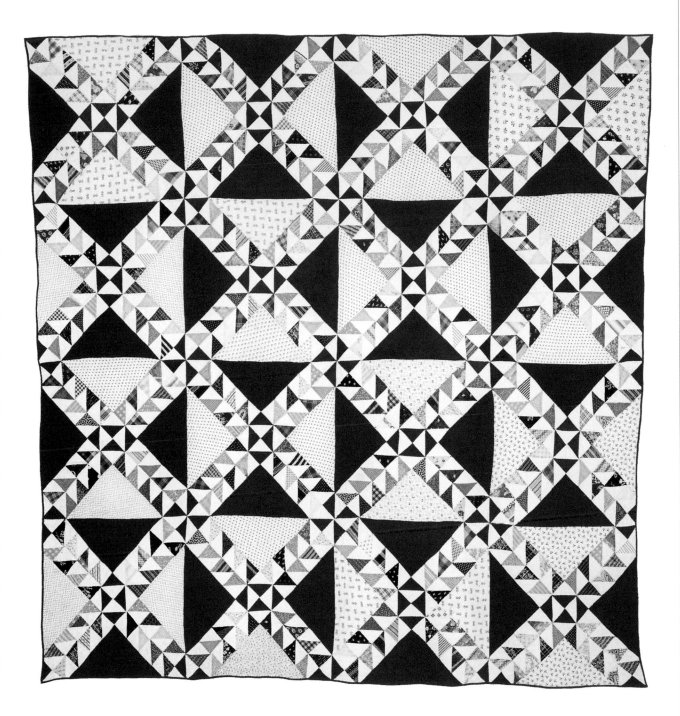

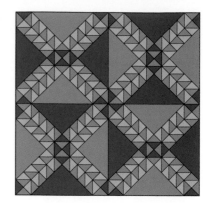
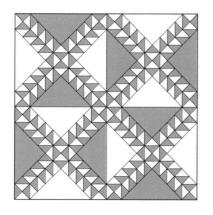

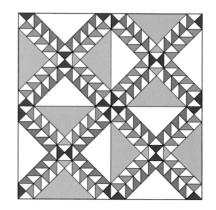

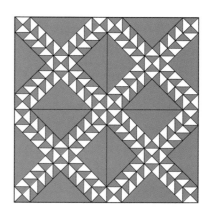

Photocopy this page, then create your own color scheme using colored pencils or markers. Refer to the examples on the previous pages, or design a unique arrangement to match your decor or please your fancy.

I f you vary the setting angle from diagonal to straight, add sashing, or change the alternation of light and dark fabrics, you can create many intriguing allover patterns from the Lady of the Lake block. Note how different the pattern looks with plain or pieced alternate blocks. These variations may change the size of the quilt; you could compensate by using more or fewer blocks or adding borders.

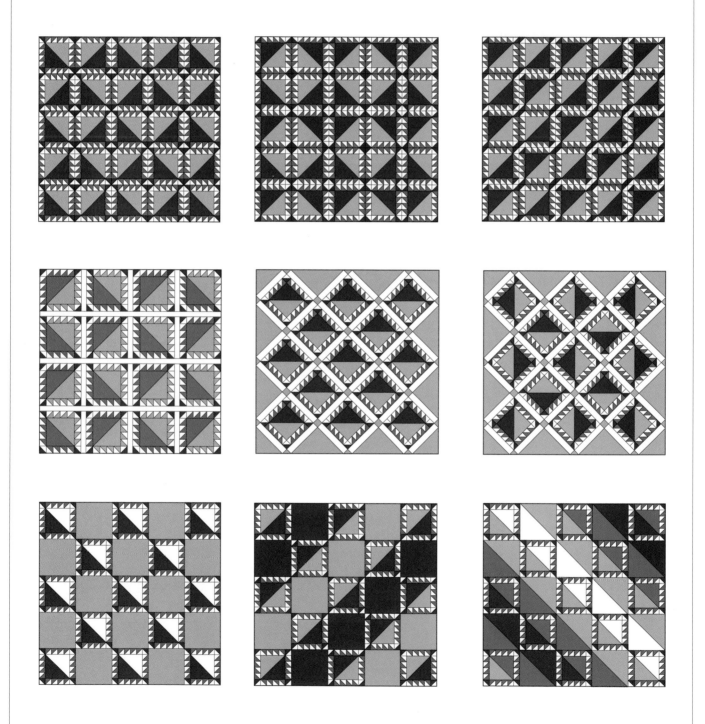

Rocky Glen Quilt

If you change the orientation of the small triangle squares for each block as shown, you will have a Rocky Glen block. In the quilt pictured here, the number and size of the blocks are different from ours, but you can use our instructions and this lovely antique as an inspiration for making your own unique variation.

Change the set from diagonal to straight and add a single border of small pieced squares to create symmetrical framing of the larger pieced squares. You can also arrange the blocks (and half-blocks) in the same manner as for our quilt. (See also "Changing Colors," page 81, for more great suggestions.)

Use the chart below to plan a straight-set Rocky Glen (or Lady of the Lake) quilt.

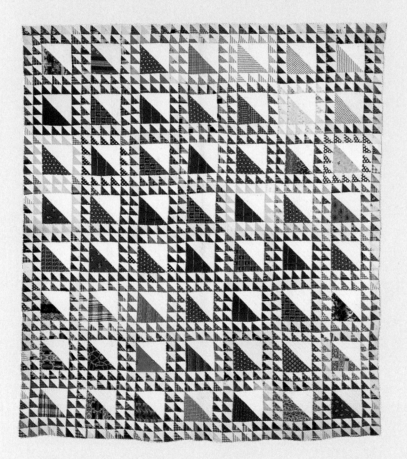

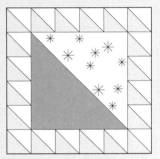

WHOLE BLOCK

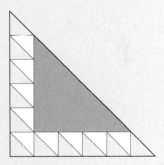

DARK HALF-BLOCK

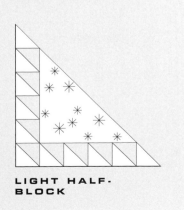

LIGHT HALF-BLOCK

STRAIGHT SETS			
Number of Blocks	Block Layout	Size without Border	Size with One Border
25	5″ × 5″	67½″ square	72″ square
36	6″ × 6″	81″ square	85½″ square
49	7″ × 7″	94½″ square	99″ square
64	8″ × 8″	108″ square	112½″ square

Sonora Springtime: A Mirage

BY AURELIE DWYER STACK,
HAND-QUILTED BY MARJORIE DOWNS

This magical wallhanging was begun in a workshop called Star Gardens; it is based on the traditional Trailing Star block. Space does not permit us to give complete step-by-step directions here, but this quilt is too lovely not to share—whether for your admiration or emulation—so we challenge you to follow our abbreviated guide. Experienced quilters will find that with a bit of planning, the block is really not difficult to draft or assemble.

SQUARE #1

SQUARE #2

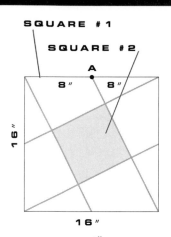

A

8″ 8″

1 6 ″

16″

SQUARE #3

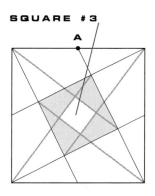

A

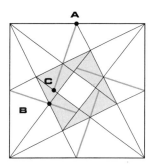

A

C

B

1. Draw a 16″ square (Square #1). Mark the center of each side (A). Connect A's and corners as shown, forming Square #2.

2. Connect corners of Squares #1 and #2 as shown, completing large star points and forming Square #3.

3. Use points A and B to line up ruler, then mark only from A to C, completing one small star point. Complete remaining three small star points in the same manner.

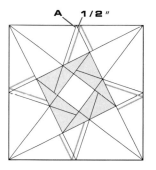

A 1/2″

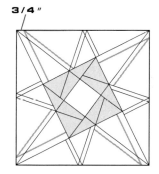

3/4″

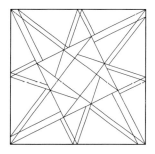

4. Mark a point ½″ to the right of A on upper side of Square #1. Beginning at marks, draw lines parallel to edges of small star point, ending at edge of Square #2. Repeat on remaining three sides.

5. Mark a point ¾″ to the right of upper left corner of Square #1. Mark lines parallel to edges of large star point. Repeat on remaining three sides, completing the block pattern.

FINISHED BLOCK PATTERN

14 BLOCK TEMPLATES

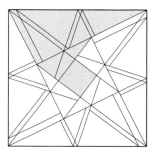

6. Draft patterns for border templates, referring to Finished Quilt diagram.

7. Use patterns to make 14 window templates for block and 2 for border patches.

8. Cut out and piece 2 blocks and 2 reversed blocks, plus 4 border strips.

9. Arrange blocks and reversed blocks as shown, rotating blocks on lower row.

10. Join blocks, then add border with mitered corners, to complete quilt top.

BLOCK

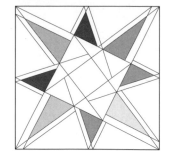

REVERSED BLOCK

REVERSED BLOCK ROTATED 180°

BLOCK ROTATED 180°

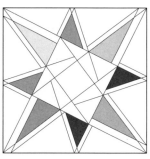

FINISHED QUILT

GREAT IDEA

Aurelie Stack was inspired by the Sonora desert in spring, with its cactus flowers and waves of heat and light. It is the careful choice and placement of color and pattern on the quilt that give it such a wonderful shimmering effect. Note how lighter values in the center and darker ones in the corners give the feeling of a mirage, which is enhanced by the use of hand-dyed fabrics and the right and wrong sides of several prints, so there seems to be a haze over the surface.

When you want to utilize a specific part of your fabric for a specific effect on your quilt, mark the pieces using transparent or window templates: Arrange the templates over your fabric, isolating the motif or color you want, and mark your patches one at a time. It will take a little longer, and may require more fabric, but the effect will be well worth the effort.

Photocopy this page, then create your own color scheme using colored pencils or markers. Refer to the examples on the previous pages, or design a unique arrangement to match your decor or please your fancy.

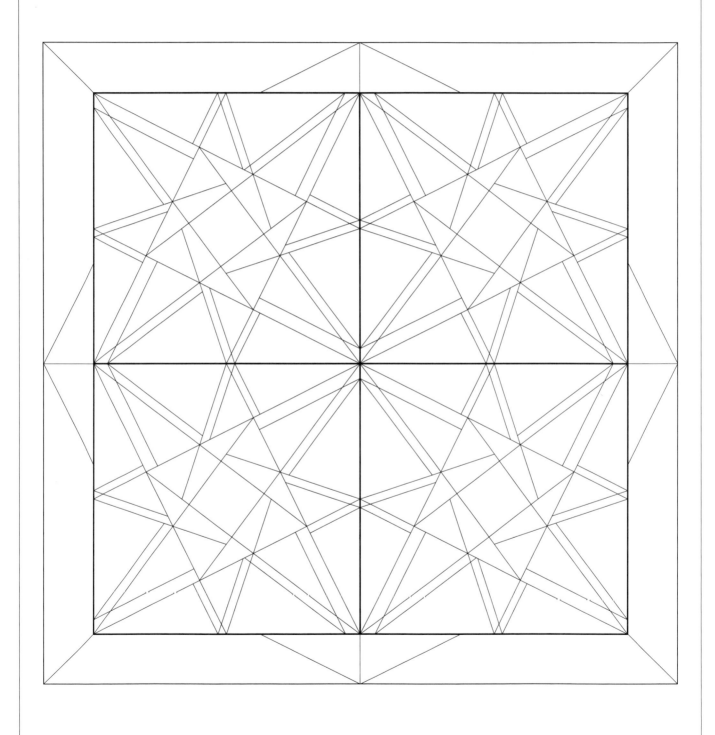

Appendix

The sample cutting charts and schematics below demonstrate how these elements work together to provide the information needed to cut most of the pieces for any quilt project in this book. Any additional cuts, such as for binding, can be found in the "Fabric and Cutting List" for each project.

DRAFTING SCHEMATIC ———————————
Drafting schematics, which do not include seam allowance, are provided for your convenience as an aid for preparing templates.

DRAFTING SCHEMATIC
(No seam allowance added)

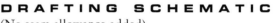
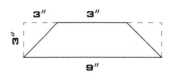

CUTTING SCHEMATIC ———————————
Cutting schematics, which include seam allowance, can be used for preparing templates (with seam allowance included) but are given primarily as an aid for speed-cutting shapes using a rotary cutter and special rulers with angles marked on them.

CUTTING SCHEMATICS
(Seam allowance included)

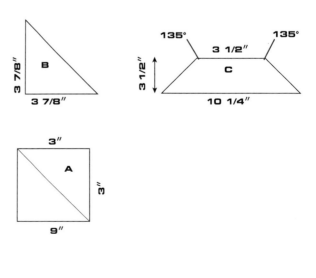

FABRIC AND YARDAGE
This column gives the color and amount of fabric needed to cut groups of shapes, rounded up to the next ¼ yard. To change the color scheme of a project, refer to the dimensions given for individual groups of shapes and combine them as needed to calculate the new yardage.

FIRST CUT
Cut the number of pieces in the sizes indicated on either the lengthwise or crosswise grain unless otherwise stated, using templates or rotary cutting rulers. For 40″-long strips, cutting completely across the width of the fabric usually provides the most economical cuts.

SECOND CUT
Cut the number of pieces in the sizes and/or shapes indicated, referring to the cutting schematics for angles and cut sizes. Reversed pieces are designated by a subscript $_R$ (e.g., the reverse of a B patch is designated B_R) and can frequently be obtained from the same strips as their mirror images by cutting the two shapes alternately.

	FIRST CUT		SECOND CUT	
Fabric and Yardage	Number of Pieces	Size	Number of Pieces	Shape
PLAIN PATCHES				
Red Solid ¼ yd.	1	3⅞″ × 20″	8	A
	1	3½″ × 40″	8	B
White Solid ¼ yd.	1	3⅞″ × 20″	8	A
	1	3½″ × 40″	6	C
SPEEDY TRIANGLE SQUARES				
Red Solid and White Solid ½ yd. each	2	16½″ × 20⅝″	72	B/B[1]
BORDER				
Blue Checked ½ yd.	2	2½″ × 29″		
	2	2½″ × 32″		

[1]See Speedy Triangle Squares (page 93). Mark 4 × 5 grids with 3⅞″ squares.

8 RED SOLID A'S
From ¼ yd. red solid, cut one 3⅞″ × 20″ strip. From strip cut four 3⅞″ squares. Cut squares in half to make 8 right-triangle A's.

6 WHITE SOLID C'S
From ¼ yd. white solid cut one 3½″ × 40″ strip. From strip cut six trapezoids.

BORDER
From ½ yd. blue checked cut two 2½″ × 29″ and two 2½″ × 32″ border strips.

FOOTNOTE
Use the cited instructions for Speedy Triangle Squares and mark the grids in the layout indicated.

APPLIQUÉS
From ¼ yd. red floral cut 16 flowers and 8 buds. From ¼ yd. blue floral cut 56 leaves.

FOOTNOTE REFERENCE
See the footnote underneath the chart for additional information about cutting this group of shapes.

APPLIQUÉS		
Fabric and Yardage	Number of Pieces	Shape
Red Floral ¼ yd.	16	Flower
	8	Bud
Blue Floral ¼ yd.	56	Leaf

Speedy Triangle Squares

1. Cut matching pieces of two contrasting fabrics (see individual project directions for dimensions).

  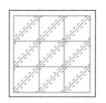 

2. Mark a square grid on wrong side of lighter-color fabric, leaving ½″ margin all around grid. Mark half as many grid squares as triangle squares needed; each marked square will make two pieced squares. (NOTE: Mark grid squares ⅞″ larger than desired finished size of triangle squares.)

3. Mark diagonals across squares.

4. Pin marked fabric to contrasting fabric, right sides together. Stitch ¼″ from each diagonal, on both sides of line.

5. Cut along marked lines, grid lines first and then diagonals.

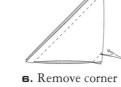

6. Remove corner stitches.

7. Open triangles. Press seams toward darker fabric.

Successful Seams

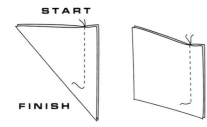

START

FINISH

◆ *Sewing acute angles (less than 90°):* Start at end with larger corner angle and stitch across piece to end with acute angle. (NOTE: Stitching into seam allowance is not advisable at acute angles. Unless the seam allowance is left free, it may be difficult to align adjacent edges that have not yet been stitched.)

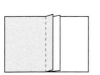 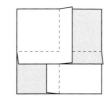 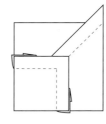

◆ *For seams pressed toward lighter fabric:* Trim darker seam allowance to ⅛″, to prevent it from extending beyond lighter seam allowance and showing through on right side.

◆ *For intersections of seams:* Press seams away from each other, either open or to one side. (NOTE: At intersections of four or more pieces, press all seams either clockwise or counterclockwise.)

◆ *For set-in seams:* Press the joining seam(s) of the outer pieces to one side. Press seam allowances of the set-in piece flat, toward the outer pieces.

Shoemaker's Puzzle Quilt
(pages 44 to 53)

ACTUAL-SIZE PATTERNS

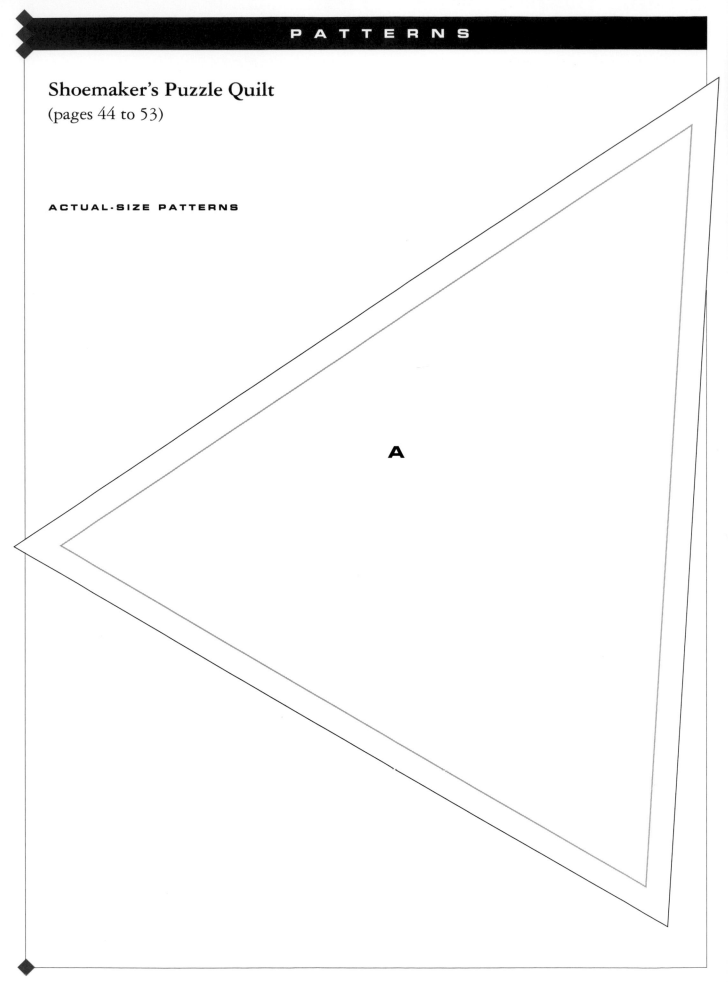

A

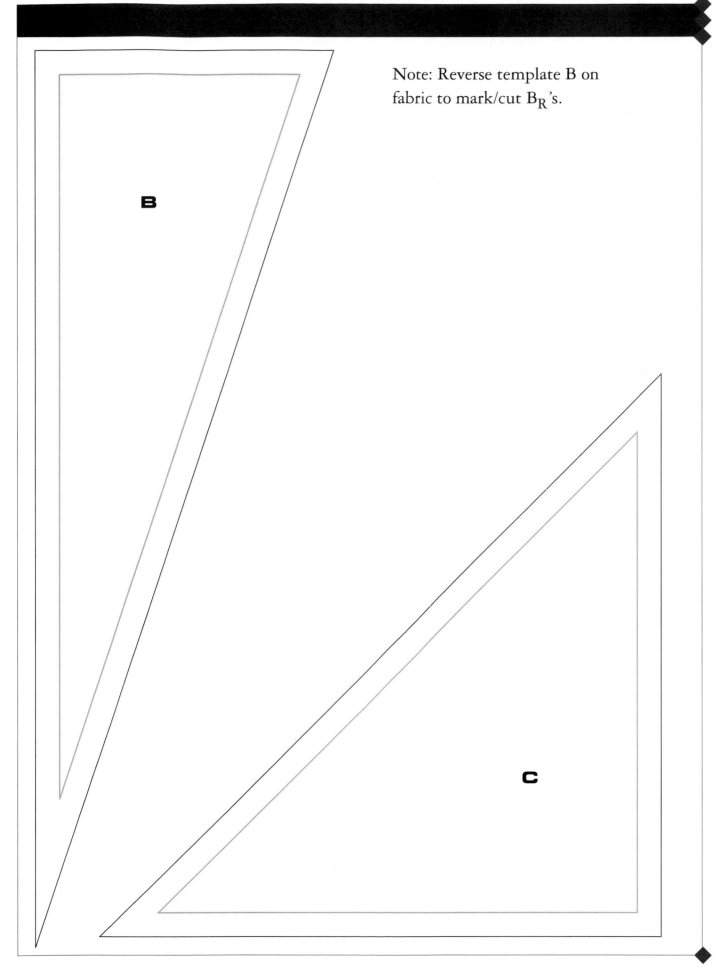

Note: Reverse template B on fabric to mark/cut B$_R$'s.

B

C

Starry Path Pillow
(pages 18 to 25)

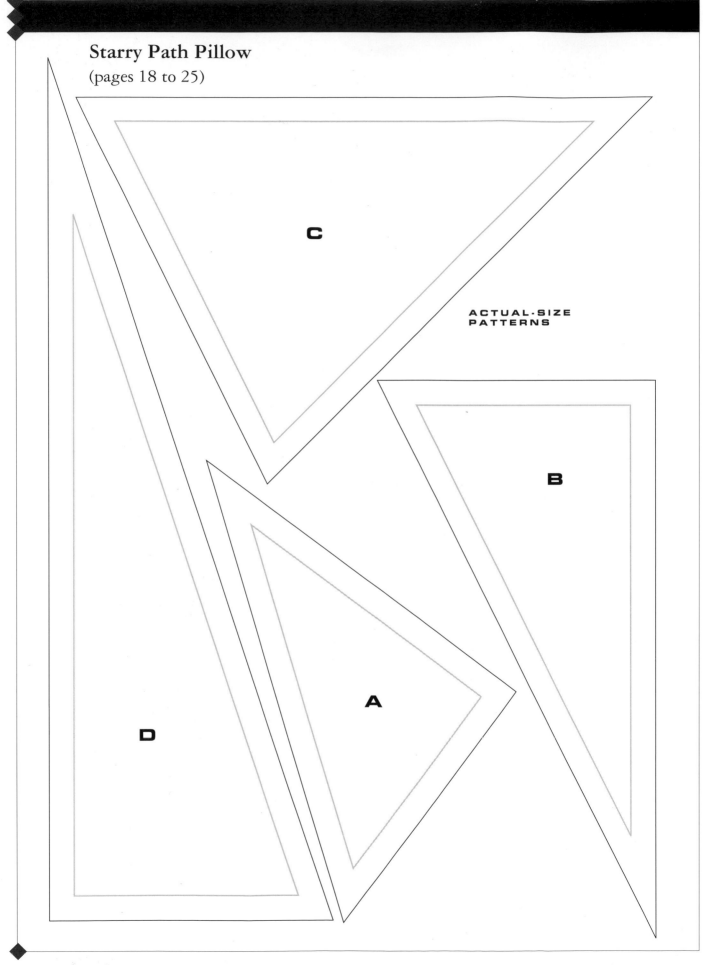

C

ACTUAL-SIZE
PATTERNS

B

A

D